Among the Giants

Among the Giants

A Year at Kew's Arboretum

Carolyn Fry and Christina Harrison

First published in Great Britain in 2025 by Gaia, an imprint of
Octopus Publishing Group Ltd
Carmelite House
50 Victoria Embankment
London EC4Y 0DZ
www.octopusbooks.co.uk
www.octopusbooksusa.com

An Hachette UK Company
www.hachette.co.uk

The authorized representative in the EEA is Hachette Ireland, 8 Castlecourt Centre, Dublin 15, D15 XTP3, Ireland (email: info@hbgi.ie)

Text Copyright © Carolyn Fry and Christina Harrison 2025
Trademark Copyright © The Board of Trustees of the Royal Botanic Gardens, Kew 2025
Design and Layout Copyright © Octopus Publishing Group Ltd 2025

Distributed in the US by Hachette Book Group
1290 Avenue of the Americas, 4th and 5th Floors
New York, NY 10104

Distributed in Canada by Canadian Manda Group
664 Annette St., Toronto, Ontario, Canada M6S 2C8

All rights reserved. No part of this work may be reproduced or utilized in any form or by any means, electronic or mechanical, including photocopying, recording or by any information storage and retrieval system, without the prior written permission of the publisher.

Carolyn Fry and Christina Harrison assert the moral right
to be identified as the authors of this work.

ISBN: 978-1-85675-567-2
eISBN: 978-1-85675-568-9

A CIP catalogue record for this book is available from the British Library.

Typeset in 12/21pt Plantin MT Pro by Six Red Marbles UK, Thetford, Norfolk.

Printed and bound in Great Britain.

1 3 5 7 9 10 8 6 4 2

Commissioning Editor: Jessica Minocha
Editor: Scarlet Furness
Copy Editor: Susanne Hillen
Creative Director: Mel Four
Production Controller: Sarah Parry

This FSC® label means that materials used for the product have been responsibly sourced.

For

Geoff Harrison

(23 July 1940 – 3 March 2024)

Christina's father

And

Avril Jane Fry

(5 October 1944 – 17 June 2024)

Carolyn's mother

Who taught us both the power of stories and a love of the natural world.

Nature's peace will flow into you
as sunshine flows into trees.
John Muir

Contents

Preface	ix
Part One: Spring	1
Part Two: Summer	67
Part Three: Autumn	117
Part Four: Winter	183
Selected Reading	251
Index	255
Acknowledgements	269
About Kew Gardens	271
Picture Credits	273

Preface

Kew's Arboretum sits within a landscape that is rich in cultural history. It has undergone many changes, from a wild riverside to royal pleasure grounds to a world-class scientific collection. Over the past 266 years, trees and shrubs from around the temperate world have been collected and planted together here in related groups by successive teams of gardeners and arborists. The result is a unique collection and landscape, rich with stories.

Today, Kew's Arboretum covers much of the Garden's 130 hectares (320 acres). It offers a valuable scientific and horticultural resource of around 2,000 species representing the temperate forests of the world, from the familiar to the incredibly rare. But the Arboretum is also invaluable in helping us to reconnect with nature and learn about the environment and its need for its protection. Trees are precious natural resources and key assets in the fight against climate change, but they are also natural wonders in themselves, and ones which deserve to be celebrated.

I (Carolyn) feel very at home in Kew Gardens, having worked here regularly for two decades. My first book assignment came in 2006 when I was asked to write *The World of Kew* to accompany the ten-part BBC 2 TV Series *A New Year at Kew*. My research for the book encompassed delving into the archives to explore the Garden's history, interviewing staff and even visiting the Caribbean island of Montserrat to learn how Kew scientists were helping to create a new botanic garden following the destruction of the previous one in a volcanic eruption. It gave me a fabulous insight into the diverse nature of Kew's work, as well as the role its plant collectors played in shaping colonial history.

I went on to work on more books in collaboration with the Gardens, through which I shared stories on botanical exploration, the work of the Millennium Seed Bank at Wakehurst (Kew's sister garden in West Sussex), and the importance of seeds to humanity. I contributed articles to *Kew* magazine, on everything from medicinal plants to Kew's work to find new coffee-yielding species that might tolerate

PREFACE

conditions forecast under climate change. And, in 2020 and 2023, I wrote texts for two of Kew's 'State of the World's Plants and Fungi' reports. But an aspect of the Garden's work I'd not covered much was its trees, which spurred my collaboration with Christina Harrison.

I (Christina) have been privileged enough to work at Kew for 25 years, most recently researching for a PhD on the history of the Arboretum. In that time, I have come to know the Arboretum and certain specimen trees very well, and certainly have my favourites, but there are always things that surprise me every time I wander its many pathways. The sheer diversity and seasonality of this landscape continues to inspire and delight. From the burst of colour from the magnolias and cherries in spring, followed by the blooms of the horse chestnuts, *Catalpa* and *Paulownia* among many others, through the green splendour of summer, to the glorious autumnal colours and fruits, berries, seeds and cones, each season in the Arboretum offers its own highlights. These visual feasts are the public-facing spectacles that I and many other visitors love, but behind the scenes is a wealth of knowledge that I really admire.

The people who look after these valuable botanical specimens are very special too. They work high among the wide canopies of Kew's cathedral of trees, in a verdant world of elevated vistas, and are inheritors of a wealth of knowledge that has been built over successive generations of Kew's gardeners and arborists. One of the joys of writing this book has been spending time with a team of people who genuinely understand the huge range of tree species they are working with and the science behind what they do. Not only do they respect the history of the place they work in, and those that have gone before, but they also take on the responsibility to build on that legacy to ensure that Kew's trees will be around for a long time to come.

Meeting this team – Kew's Tree Gang – and understanding their work has been a real privilege and seeing how they approach this historic but dynamic collection has been a revelation. Their work carries on an age-old tradition of plant husbandry, and centuries of arboricultural skills development, to grow and understand the true nature of a tree. The variety of tasks, knowledge, research and outreach they embrace will hopefully be as fascinating to you as it was to us. As they face the challenges of managing this important tree collection in a changing climate, they will surely be remembered for meeting that challenge head on.

Part One

SPRING

On a clear April morning, high in a large beech tree, lime-green spring leaves are unfolding from slim pointed buds. This is a European beech (*Fagus sylvatica*), a tree common across southern England where its elegant form and lofty status have crowned it the 'queen of the woods'. The tree's bright new growth contrasts with the glossy dark evergreen leaves of the holly (*Ilex*) trees that surround it, and which are often natural neighbours to beech in England's wild woods. At its base, hoverflies seek out the new-season nectar from white umbrellas of cow parsley and the nodding heads of English bluebells. Their fragrance, which mingles on the warming air, carries with it the promise of spring after the bitter winds of winter.

Despite appearances, however, this beech is not growing in a wild ecosystem. Rather, it and its prickly neighbours form a small ornamental glade within the Royal Botanic Gardens, Kew, in west London. Around it are species of horse chestnuts or buckeyes *(Aesculus)*, hickories (*Carya*), oaks (*Quercus*), walnuts (*Juglans*), limes *(Tilia),* and more unfamiliar trees such as the Caucasian nettle tree (*Celtis caucasica)* and the delightfully named wedge-leaved bubble flower (*Meliosma cuneifolia*). Together, they are constituents of the world's most diverse collection of living plants, which includes 11,000 trees representing more than 2,000 species. In this Arboretum, which stretches across two-thirds of the 130-hectare (320-acre) site, are trees of all ages and sizes, originating from countries across the temperate world. They have been gathered together over several centuries for the benefit of science, education and pleasure.

Among the oldest trees are the 'Old Lions', which include a maidenhair tree *(Ginkgo biloba)* and a Japanese pagoda tree (*Styphnolobium japonicum*) both native to China, as well as a black locust tree (*Robinia pseudoacacia*) and a cucumber tree (*Magnolia accuminata*) from North America, and an oriental plane (*Platanus orientalis*) from south-eastern Europe, all planted in the late 18th century. The Gardens' tallest tree is a coast redwood (*Sequoia sempervirens*), its height matching that of a 13-storey building. And the luckiest might just be a Corsican pine (*Pinus nigra* subspecies *laricio*), which has so far survived a direct hit by a light aircraft in 1928, whereby the pilot parachuted to safety, and not one but two lightning strikes.

In this managed living collection, as in nature, fate favours some trees more than others. As the new year delivers rising sap and a spurt of growth for most specimens in the Arboretum, the holly-encircled beech is coming to the end of its days. Despite having grown here robustly in its glade for several decades, it has lately begun to lean, and low on its smooth grey trunk it has developed a long bitumen-like stain that hints it has succumbed to a fungal infection. For the safety of visitors to the Gardens, it will have to be taken down. Removing a tree is not necessarily a bad thing, however, as it allows space for other specimens to grow, creates more light for herbaceous plants below, opens views, and allows for consideration of what else might be planted to enhance the beauty and value of the area.

Kew has been evolving since its inception in the early 1700s, when Prince Frederick, son of King George II and Queen Caroline, leased Kew Park, next to his parents' Richmond estate beside the River Thames. This was a time when European explorers were undertaking scientific voyages of discovery, mapping territories unknown to Western societies, and beginning to learn about the vast diversity of plants and animals on Earth. Frederick was deeply interested in science and botany and wanted to create a botanic garden as part of his newly landscaped estate. After his early death in 1751, his wife Princess Augusta fulfilled his plans in his memory, developing 14 hectares (34.5 acres) of land, of which a portion was a dedicated botanic garden and tree collection over 3.6 hectares (9 acres). A decade of intense landscaping and planting followed.

Princess Augusta was advised by her friend the politician and plant enthusiast John Stuart, the third Earl of Bute, and employed a curator named William Aiton in 1759 to manage the royal 'physick garden'. This is taken to be the founding point for today's Kew Gardens. Stuart brought many trees from the nursery and estate, in Whitton, of his late uncle the Duke of Argyll. In his day, the duke had been an avid tree collector, even being nicknamed the 'tree-monger' by the English writer and politician Horace Walpole. Many trees from Whitton were planted at Kew in 1762 – among them, some of the Old Lions that still stand today. These were planted alongside new species given as gifts or bought from nurseries, such as the ginkgo and the Japanese pagoda tree, which had been acquired from James Gordon, an early specialist in importing trees from China and Japan to meet landowners' growing demand for 'exotics'.

In 1802, Princess Augusta and Frederick's oldest son, now King George III, combined the Kew and Richmond gardens to form a large single estate. When Princess Augusta died in 1772, the king had asked the wealthy naturalist Joseph Banks to supervise the 'physick garden'. Banks had become something of a celebrity when he had returned laden with plant specimens after circumnavigating the world with explorer and cartographer James Cook on HMB *Endeavour*. Banks took this as an opportunity to create an unrivalled collection for the king, full of rare, novel and economically useful plants – including trees. Taking advantage of the rapid development of European empires and trade, Banks began sending out botanists to collect specimens exclusively for Kew. These included Francis Masson in South Africa, William Kerr in China and Allan Cunningham in Australia. The number and range of foreign plants available to British gardens had increased exponentially in this period, as European exploration in places such as Australia, North and South America, and the Himalayan regions increased. As historian Keith Alcorn explains: 'The formation of plant collections in Britain took place in the context of imperial expansion, global competition for the discovery of new botanical resources and the emergence of a transnational botanical community.' From fewer than 3,400 'exotic introductions' at Kew in 1770, by 1813 there were 11,000, and Kew had turned into a botanical treasure garden.

Following the deaths of both Banks and the king in 1820, Kew Gardens fell out of royal favour. In 1840, it was given to the British government to be turned into a public botanic garden. It was an auspicious moment. This shift from royal to national botanic garden had been promoted by Scottish garden writer and designer John Claudius Loudon who had also widely encouraged the idea of designed tree collections to be planted for education, research and public well-being. He first used the term 'arboretum' in 1806, but explored the concept thoroughly in his 1838 eight-volume illustrated book *Arboretum et Fruticetum Britannicum; Or, The Trees and Shrubs of Britain* (completed with help from Kew's then curator John Smith) where he proclaimed that trees were some of the most important things that could be introduced to a country for either timber or ornament. He aimed high – encouraging the planting of arboreta with every known tree hardy in the British climate, ideally arranged in taxonomic order (according to how botanists classified them), and clearly labelled for everyone to see.

William Hooker, who became the first director of Kew in its guise as the new national botanic garden, also wanted an expansive tree collection. At a time when Britain's burgeoning middle class was embracing recreation, and Kew was becoming a testing ground for plants that might yield commodities of use to the British Empire, Hooker's desire was for the Gardens to be both attractive and useful. After being granted large additional tracts of the old royal pleasure grounds in the 1850s, he worked with landscape architect William Andrews Nesfield to create a plan in which trees would be planted ornamentally and taxonomically to make Kew a site of both beauty and science. Nesfield also drove wide vistas through the landscape, to carry visitors out from the newly built Palm House into the Gardens, and to provide long-ranging views of the Pagoda (a Chinese-style folly that had been built for Princess Augusta) and the River Thames. When Joseph Hooker succeeded his father William in 1865, he too left his mark on the Arboretum. He created a large pinetum at the southern end of the Gardens (at the time the largest collection of conifers in the world) and planted Cedar Vista and other avenues.

The practice initiated by Joseph Banks of sending plant collectors abroad to gather exotic specimens had continued well into the 19th century, facilitated by the expanding British Empire. Plants new to Britain, packaged as seeds or bulbs, began to arrive in their hundreds. Then, with the 1833 invention of a sealed portable glasshouse known as a Wardian case, live plants could be transported by ship, protected from sea spray. Thereafter, exciting novel species began to arrive at Kew in a steady stream, among them many trees that found their way into the Arboretum. New cherries (*Prunus*) and maples (*Acer*) arrived from East Asia, conifers from India and America, *Eucalyptus* and *Acacia* from Australia, southern beech (*Nothofagus*) from South America and oaks (*Quercus*) from Mexico, alongside countless others. The Pinetum and oak collection were to become particularly extensive in the late 19th century.

Kew's modern-day Arboretum still carries the echoes of past eras and places. In the main part of the Arboretum, south of the iconic Victorian Palm House, are collections of trees arranged by botanical family and genus. The Hookers had designed the landscape in this way in the late 19th century to help botanists study and classify trees that were related to each other, and to teach others how to identify them and to appreciate how different species grew. Today, the largest tree collections include those from North America, Europe and the Caucasus, China, Taiwan, Korea and Japan. The oak collection is by far the largest genus represented in the Arboretum as part of a large area planted with members of the beech family (Fagaceae) of which oaks are a part. These are followed in number by hollies, maples and pines (*Pinus*). But there are also collections of limes (*Tilia*), ash (*Fraxinus*), Indian bean trees (*Catalpa*), horse chestnuts (*Aesculus*), trees in the legume family (Fabaceae), and many, many more.

A walk through Kew's Arboretum in spring reveals the 'pink tulip tree' Campbell's magnolia (*Magnolia campbellii*), native to India, China and Myanmar, alight with brilliant cerise blooms in the Magnolia Glade. In nearby Cherry Walk, and around the Rose Garden, myriad delicate petals of multiple Japanese cherry trees swirl like pink snow on the breeze. And next to the Waterlily House, the rare sapphire dragon tree (*Paulownia kawakamii*) from China shows off its new crop of vibrant foxglove-like flowers. It is a place of botanical wonders.

The Arboretum's extraordinary trees have been celebrated in many ways before, but the work and the majority of people who maintain this world-renowned collection have so far remained out of the public eye. The amount of technical and scientific work that goes into managing Kew's arboreal giants through the seasons is surprising. The Arboretum is an evolving landscape, in which new trees are planted and failing or diseased ones are taken away in a constant process of landscape management. It is the overarching responsibility of a specialist arboricultural team, known as the Tree Gang, to undertake such work. Their job is to balance caring for the ancient trees, and maintaining the historic landscape features, with planting new collections and meeting the demands of Kew as a modern botanic garden and world-class scientific institution, one that welcomes nearly two and a half million visitors every year. Critically, the Tree Gang must also ensure that the Gardens can continue fulfilling these varied roles well into the future, after their time in the Arboretum is over.

In this capacity, the seven-strong team face an entirely new challenge unknown to their forbears. This is climate change, which, through higher temperatures, less predictable rainfall and more intense storms, is putting the UK's trees – including those at Kew – under great pressure. There is no doubt that the UK is heating up, as its ten warmest years on record have all occurred since 2002. Future predictions are for warmer winters, hotter summers, and more frequent and severe extreme weather events. According to Forest Research, the UK's principal organization for forestry and tree-related research, British woodlands will face increasing risks from droughts, flooding, pests, disease, wind and fire. Among the nation's most susceptible trees are beeches, which have shallow root systems. Those in southern England are particularly at risk due to the lower rainfall and higher temperatures already being experienced there.

The specimen of European beech that the Tree Gang is

set to cut down may well be a victim of this human-induced phenomenon. Once stressed, such as by prolonged periods of hot, dry weather, beeches' defence mechanisms against pathogens decrease. The tell-tale jet-black growth creeping its way up the bark of this tree is indicative of the brittle cinder fungus (*Kretzschmaria deusta*). This common fungus is aggressive and well known for inhabiting temperate hardwood trees such as beech. It stealthily 'soft rots' both the lignin and cellulose at the heart of the tree, often creating dangerous instability in its structure while the canopy still appears full and healthy. There is no official treatment for this fungus and the prognosis is, sadly, terminal. Where such a tree is growing next to a well-used visitor path, as in this case, its days are inevitably limited. Although this beech is not part of the scientific collection of *Fagus* in the Gardens, it has been a valued ornamental specimen and its absence will be felt in this usually quiet corner.

The felling will be undertaken by four members of the Tree Gang: Tom Fry, the arboricultural supervisor, along with arborists Jamie Slessor, Rich Church and Will Harding. As it will take a couple of days to complete the task, Tom has already notified the Visitor Operations team so that the public can be alerted. The path beside which the beech stands is a major thoroughfare, linking Kew's Japanese Gateway, or Chokushi-Mon, (a replica of a gate at the Western Temple of the Original Vow in Kyoto, Japan) in the south to a five-way intersection of paths that connects to the Victoria Gate entrance in the east, the Orangery Café and the Elizabeth Gate entrance in the north, and the Lake in the west. To prevent any visitors getting too close to the action, Tom unwinds green temporary fencing to physically block the way and sets up a triangular 'Tree Cutting' warning sign beside it. With the team starting early – it is still only 8am – they have two hours in which to make headway before visitors start coming through the gates. As they begin work, grey squirrels scurry for cover.

The Tree Gang are used to getting such a site set up and work companionably together in the spring sunshine, gathering the tools they need, checking ropes and kit, and chatting away about the tree and the task in hand. Twenty-five-year-old Jamie, who is to work in the canopy lopping the branches, is the youngest member of the Gang. He obtained a degree in music technology before deciding that being shut indoors for long hours in a windowless, soundproof studio wasn't for him. After spending a year working for a company that removed Japanese knotweed and other invasive weeds, and as someone who liked plants and enjoyed rock climbing, the idea of being an arborist appealed. Then, while wandering among Kew's historic tree collections on his 22nd birthday, Jamie realized it would be a brilliant place to be an arborist. Within months he had secured a place on the Kew Arboricultural Apprenticeship – a two-year, full-time course – and he was lucky enough to be offered a permanent role soon after graduating. Since then, he has been climbing trees at Kew almost every day.

Today, he sets to work securing two ropes as climbing lines from discrete anchor points on strong central branches high in the beech. The primary line is yellow, the back-up one purple, so they can be easily distinguished. He then anchors a separate thick green rigging line, complete with pulley, to be used for lowering timber to the ground. In no time, Jamie has ascended his primary rope and is in place on a low branch, electric chainsaw in hand, ready to start work. At the bottom of the tree, meanwhile, Rich has cut a large rectangle of bark from the trunk and affixed in its place a winch – of the kind used by sailors to sheet-in and release sails – on a sturdy metal plate. Rich and Tom secure it tightly in place with a strap that wraps around the trunk. With a heavy-duty Makita electric drill replacing the sailors' standard manual handle, the team will use the winch to lower particularly large branches in a controlled way. These will then be carried to the bright red wood-chipping machine that has been towed into position by tractor.

With everyone set, Jamie begins work. Working from the bottom up, he clears small branches in the canopy to make space for lowering larger limbs later. The high-pitched whirr of the electric chainsaw begins, and a thin branch hits the ground with a light 'thunk'. More small leafy branches follow, accompanied by a snow of falling wood dust. As Jamie edges towards the tree's farthermost twigs to make these early cuts, the branches dip under his weight, and it is clear why the term 'going out on limb' denotes a risky move. But, confident in his equipment, experience and abilities, Jamie moves deftly around the tree, pausing between cuts to reposition his ropes and make himself secure. As the screaming chainsaw slices through the wood, he drops small to medium branches, and ties larger ones to the rigging line to be winched down. On the ground, Rich, Tom and Will chop up the timber as necessary and drag it to the wood chipper. Gritty cracks and shots punctuate the machine's rumble, as wood fed into a chute is chewed at speed by the spinning blades within.

Throughout the day, as the tree is methodically reduced in size, visitors come and watch the proceedings from the barrier, interested in what the team are doing. Jamie admits that cutting a tree down in front of a crowd can be unnerving – especially if that crowd is of young children with a passion for saving the environment and preserving forests. 'We've been heckled by schoolchildren and called tree murderers in the past,' he says, confessing that such a response can be somewhat disheartening when the Tree Gang are taking a tree out for good reason, such as today. But he feels that this is a small price to pay for work that is otherwise a highly enjoyable mix of the practical and the cerebral. 'I really enjoy the fact that our work is so varied,' he says. 'On the one hand you have to think about the biological aspects of the tree and how things such as the weather or pests or the soil conditions might be affecting it. And then there are aspects such as health and safety, and the practicalities of how you climb a tree and work in it in an efficient way.'

Climbing a tree safely calls for particular equipment and techniques, with regulations dictating certain practices. The UK Health and Safety Regulations call for the use of two climbing ropes between 10mm and 14mm wide, each anchored to separate points in the tree, and climbers must carry a personal first-aid kit on their harness. A wide array of equipment is available to arborists to help them work effectively. As a minimum, the tree-climbing professional's kit will probably include: two ropes (and a bag to store them in); their harness with a bridge onto which the two rope systems connect; a friction device, which will either stop or allow rope to pass through it; a selection of three-way-locking connectors called carabiners; a positioning lanyard, used to temporarily hold a climber in position; climbing spikes that can help the climber achieve a solid grip when removing a tree; and a cambium saver. The last of these is a device that prevents ropes from damaging the tree, the cambium being the growing layer just beneath the bark. Then there's critical personal protective equipment, such as chainsaw-proof boots, trousers and gloves, and a helmet with eye and ear protection. Bluetooth headsets are helpful for communication between workers in the tree and those on the ground. Each arborist tends to have their own personal preferences as to what kit they use.

Various tried-and-tested techniques exist for getting ropes into a tree and then using them to climb. Purists might choose to manually throw a climbing rope directly into a tree, a method that includes coiling the rope into a bundle known as a 'granny's handbag', then throwing it up into the branches in such a way that the rope ends up looped over a strong branch, with both ends reachable from the ground. An alternative is to manually launch a thin throw line with a weighted beanbag attached to the bottom; this can be done by swinging the beanbag like a pendulum between the legs on a coil of the line and releasing it to fly up over the chosen branch. Or a more fail-safe method is to use a 'Big Shot'; a catapult on a long yellow pole capable of accurately propelling the weight high into the tree. Once the beanbag arrives back on the ground the climbing rope can be tied to it and the throw line used to pull it over the branch.

There are two main techniques that arborists use for climbing trees, namely the stationary (also single, static) rope technique (SRT) and the moving (double, dynamic) rope technique (MRT). SRT was developed more recently and is the method used most often by the Tree Gang. As it's easier on the body to climb using SRT, it is a good choice when climbing very tall trees, such as many of those at Kew. First, the rope must be secured in the tree. The Tree Gang usually use base anchors, where the non-working end of the rope is tied around the trunk close to ground level. Actually climbing the tree involves use of a foot ascender or similar device; this enables the climber to stand vertically at a fixed point on the rope, then ascend up it, one step at a time, much like climbing a combination of snake and ladder. Should the arborist need to move their anchor while working – for example, to climb higher in the tree – they use their lanyard to secure them temporarily while they untie their anchor point and fix a new one.

With the MRT, the rope is not stationary on a branch but instead runs over it in a loop. With this technique, each side of the rope is carrying 50 per cent of the climbers' weight. So, when the arborist pulls up, they're only hauling half their weight. The tree itself provides footholds, but the climber must use their leg muscles, upper body and core strength to ascend. The Tree Gang tends to use this technique to climb small trees. Because the rope moves in relation to the tree, a cambium saver must be used to protect the bark. This is usually a strip of thick webbing or other strong material with either metal rings at each end or a swivelling pulley connecting the ends. The arborist's climbing rope is threaded through the rings or pulley, so the moving rope is no longer in contact with – and therefore can't damage – the bark.

To assist with ascending and descending ropes arborists use a friction device, which has several points of contact with the rope. When the climber is clipped to the device, their weight puts enough force on two points to stop any movement down the rope. Only when the arborist physically collapses the device, releasing the pressure, does the rope pass through it, allowing the climber to move along the rope in either direction. They must do this with great care to avoid free-falling at speed down the rope. A similar device can be fashioned simply and cheaply using a short section of rope looped multiple times around to create a slide-and-grip knot or friction hitch. And whereas rock climbers often choose to climb with a slightly stretchy 'dynamic' rope that can absorb some shock in the case of a fall, the Tree Gang use 'static' ropes without stretch. This is because they're often sitting in a stationary position on the rope while working. 'And we shouldn't ever be taking any large falls that would be a shock to our system,' says Jamie.

It's not unusual for climbing arborists to enter the industry off the back of rock-climbing experience. Rich, for example, who is 46 and joined the Tree Gang in 2022, got to 'know the ropes of the climbing world' when he began rock climbing in his late teens – although it took him a long time to make the crossover into the arboricultural field. Having left college with A levels in the sciences and maths, he enrolled for a degree in mechanical engineering at University College London but found the theory-based course uninspiring and switched to working as a furniture restorer within his father's company instead. After 15 years, he decided to embrace a career change and took a 12-week intensive course in arboriculture at

Plumpton College, Brighton. As well as readying him for a career as an arborist, it turned Rich into a self-confessed tree geek. 'It changes your whole life because everywhere you go, instead of seeing blobs of green you see species of trees and it's so much more enriching,' he says.

After graduating from the course, Rich worked for a company in Tunbridge Wells, Kent, undertaking domestic tree surgery. It was brutal work, much of which involved hedge trimming rather than working with and climbing trees. After two and a half years, Rich moved back to his home city of London and began freelancing with another arborist. Now he was able to work much more with trees but this role was also demanding as he was the sole climber in the partnership and at the time he was still using the more physical MRT technique, as taught on his course. A stint as a gardener at the Horniman Museum in south-east London followed before Rich spied, applied for and was offered the job of climbing arborist at Kew. 'I climb two or three days a week now, I like to work steadily, I don't like to work super-fast; it's more sustainable,' he says.

While the British arboricultural industry employs 600,000 people and contributes more than £700 million to GDP, botanical garden arborists are in the small minority compared to commercial operators. In May, an opportunity arises for the Tree Gang to meet with other arborists working within this niche at Harcourt Arboretum, the out-of-town sister site of the University of Oxford Botanic Garden in Oxfordshire. Arboretum Curator Ben Jones has invited arborists from Kew, Westonbirt Arboretum (run by Forestry England) and University Parks (an expanse of more than 28 hectares (70 acres) in central Oxford) for a climbing day. The idea is to give the Tree Gang and other teams a chance to share knowledge, experiment with different climbing methods and get to know each other.

As well as being good for networking, the event provides the opportunity for the various arborists to understand each other's climbing approaches and techniques. Botanic garden arborists sometimes go on field trips to collect seeds from wild trees to plant back in the UK, as part of efforts to help conserve natural and genetic biodiversity. On missions like this, it is not unusual for teams from different gardens to work together and share resources, which means that sometimes they find themselves working with arborists from outside their own workplace. In such circumstances, understanding the methods and equipment the person uses and being able to trust their abilities is important. With the idea of enhancing safety when different teams work together, the day will also involve the participants practising aerial rescues.

For Cecily Withall, another member of the Tree Gang, the day is also an opportunity to meet with other women arborists, who are few and far between. Cecily herself is the first permanent female member of staff to have been employed as a climbing arborist at Kew since the 1980s. Like Jamie and Rich, she followed an indirect path to the role, spending four years working as a waitress in Edinburgh before leaving to volunteer with a friend through World Wide Opportunities on Organic Farms – otherwise known as going 'WWOOF-ing'. This ongoing movement seeks, by promoting cultural and educational exchange, to build a global community aware of ecological farming and sustainability practices. In Cecily's case, during her stays on two permaculture farms in Italy, it also opened her eyes to the possibility of working with plants. On returning home she undertook the two-year Diploma in Horticulture with Plantsmanship at the Royal Botanic Garden Edinburgh, graduating in 2019.

The course included placements throughout the Garden, including one with the tree team that involved Cecily helping to fell a huge old sweet chestnut tree (*Castanea sativa*) and turning the resulting log pile into an eco-garden. Inspired, she headed south to undertake a month of work experience with the Kew Gardens' tree team. Today, six years on, she, like Jamie, has the Kew Arboricultural Apprenticeship under her belt, and is studying for the Level 4 Diploma in Arboriculture at Merrist Wood College, Guildford. 'The team is like a big family,' she explains. 'I think that's what drew me into working here the most. In horticulture I found it a little bit lonely, because you could be sent off for the whole day on your own. I kind of need the feedback from the team; I think that being part of our little network feeds my ability to work.'

Since becoming part of the Tree Gang family, Cecily has already begun making waves in the industry. In 2023, she was awarded Young Professional Arborist of the Year by the Arboricultural Association (AA), and also spoke at the AA's 2023 ARB Show, an industry and public-facing event at Westonbirt Arboretum attended by over 6,000 showgoers and 80 exhibitors. Cecily is a keen advocate of the AA's Women in Arboriculture group, which was set up to encourage women to join the industry at entry level, support those already involved, and nurture a diverse and inclusive working environment for all. 'Opportunities are out there if you reach out for them,' says Cecily. 'But there is also still that wrongful stigma that probably won't leave for a while about testosterone-fuelled men with chainsaws. But it's so far from that here at Kew.'

After a wet few weeks at Kew Gardens, during which the Tree Gang have been busy carrying out spring tasks of 'deadwooding' (removing dead twigs and branches), lifting tree canopies to improve views across the Arboretum and taking out other trees that haven't made it through the winter, the weather turns out fine on the climbing day. As they travel in Kew's new minibus down the M40 towards Oxford, the sun is bright, glinting off the puddles in sodden fields and the white sails of Great Haseley Windmill, and accentuating yellow fields of rapeseed against the grey, lowering sky. Inside the bus, there's an atmosphere of Dad taking the kids out for the day, with everyone in high spirits. 'Dad', and today's driver, is Will, who, at 62 years old and celebrating 25 years working at the Gardens, is the oldest member of the Tree Gang.

Will discovered arboriculture relatively late in life, having spent 16 years after leaving school working as a State Registered General Nurse. Although he liked the gadgets involved with nursing – the drips and drains and catheters – he was less keen on the warm, close environment of the various London hospitals in which he worked, always preferring to be outdoors. One day, while walking in Greenwich Park with his sister and young nephew, he spied some tree surgeons and decided that he wanted their job. He spent two years studying for a Level 2 qualification in Arboriculture at Capel Manor college in Enfield, north London, before joining Kew in 1999 as, in his words, 'the tea boy'. After the responsibility of running a ward, he relished not being in charge. 'I always think of myself as a backroom boy,' he says. 'You've got adventurers who go and climb Mount Everest, but they couldn't do it without the people who make the boots for them or who look after the oxygen cylinders for them. I'm the more avuncular character here, the unit Daddy.'

After an hour or so's drive, Will pulls up in the car park at Harcourt Arboretum. As the team set off to seek out their fellow tree climbers, Harcourt's resident peacocks raise their tails in welcome, the gleaming turquoise and emerald of their feathers contrasting with the flashy pinks and oranges of Harcourt's spring show of blooming azaleas and rhododendrons. The Tree Gang make their way to two towering black pines, a short way from the car park, which are to be the focus of the day's climbing. Like Kew, Harcourt Arboretum has a long history, dating back to 1835, when Archbishop Vernon Harcourt commissioned William Sawrey Gilpin to design an 3.2 hectare (8-acre) pinetum on the site. The black pines (*Pinus nigra*) were part of this original planting. Their immense size – both are over 30 metres – means that they can take plenty of climbing equipment and climbers at once. Harcourt Arboretum Curator Ben Jones admits that, with a previous team, he has even slept high in their branches.

Ben kicks off the proceedings with a welcome chat. He and his team have already installed several ropes in the trees, which hang down from high branches like multicoloured banyan roots. Both pines have a tall single trunk, several thick near-vertical branches and many limbs at gentler angles, presenting plentiful climbing opportunities and challenges. After the introductory talk, arborists from different workplaces are gathered together in groups to encourage them to climb with people they don't know. Soon, Cecily is demonstrating SRT to some of the older male climbers who are more familiar with MRT. Later, technical arborist Chrissie Dow, the only female member present today from Westonbirt's team, practises a range of rescue scenarios at height, which, in a real-life situation, would allow an injured or unconscious arborist to be safely lowered to the ground. Clearly, with both women just as technically able as their male colleagues, gender should not be barrier to being an arborist. However, Cecily and Chrissie both admit that women face some lingering hurdles in the industry; for example, there is less choice when it comes to protective clothing. 'Some old mentalities remain but that is really changing now with the new generation of arborists who are coming through,' says Cecily.

It is, of course, not the first time that women have struggled to be fully accepted within botanical circles. In 1906, Joseph Hooker, who had spent 20 years as Kew Director after succeeding his father William in the role in 1865, commented that a career in gardening for women was 'an almost impossible thing'. Just nine years later, however, Kew curator William Watson wrote in *The Gardeners' Chronicle* about how invaluable women were in the Gardens. He wrote in particular of his admiration for the enthusiasm with which women had stepped up to take on roles there after men had signed up for military service in the Great War. He acknowledged that many women already had the necessary experience, and that they should insist on the same wages as men. 'Fifteen of them are employed at Kew, and their enthusiasm, industry and efficiency are equal to those of the average young man,' he observed. 'They work the same hours and are paid the same wages.' A staff photo taken in November 1916 shows 26 women working at Kew, and by 1917 there were 31.

In December 1918, Watson appeared to have been moved to write another piece, entitled 'Women in Horticulture', where he again encouraged others to employ women, extolling the virtues and hard work of the women gardeners at Kew, and remarking on how they were 'uplifting' the role of the 'improver' (apprentice) gardener by challenging the need for such long hours (then 6am to 6pm) and low pay. He claimed that the only reason more women were not taking up gardening careers was because of the poor conditions and unfair wages, which offered nothing but financial and social insecurity. It was a claim that men had also been making over the previous decades, to no avail. Watson was an enlightened voice of his time. However, the *Kew Guild Journal* of 1944 reveals that this essay was actually written by Kew gardener Lucy H Joshua, who had given a talk of the same title to the Kew Mutual Improvement Society on 9 November 1915 and had then passed on her notes to Watson who had sent them to *The Gardeners' Chronicle*. Although not his own words, Watson was glad to champion the intelligence, botanical education and general resilience of women gardeners, and to highlight the need to improve conditions.

Even though botany and gardening had been gaining ground as perfectly respectable paid occupations for women since the late 19th century, and Swanley Horticultural College and the Royal Horticultural Society (RHS) had been offering training and examinations in horticulture from the 1890s, it was not until the First World War that women had access to a larger range of job opportunities in well-known gardens such as Kew. As Fiona Davison has described in her recent history of women gardeners, even Swanley student Olive Harrisson, who had achieved the highest RHS exam mark in the country in 1898, was not allowed to work in the Society's own gardens at Chiswick, simply because of her gender. It is notable that William Thiselton-Dyer, successor to Joseph Hooker as Kew Director from 1885, allowed two female Swanley graduates to work at Kew in 1896, with two more joining in 1897, and others following in subsequent years. This 'experiment' created huge press interest and went on to influence other gardens and nurseries elsewhere. The interest was mainly due to the fact that Thiselton-Dyer insisted the women wear knickerbockers and dress like men, which only increased interest in them rather than helping them to blend in. Several women of the time commented on feeling like tourist attractions.

Up until the First World War, men had come to Kew for

two-year stints as 'improver gardeners'. While working they had also followed an educational and scientific curriculum of weekly lectures, at the end of which they gained certificates. Thereafter, they were expected to leave to seek new roles, such as head gardeners, elsewhere. This was also the case for the new women gardeners, although opportunities following a stint at Kew were thin on the ground.

The advent of war had opened up new prospects for women. In his unpublished memoir, Kew gardener and respected arborist William Dallimore recorded that Kew's 'decorative department', which grew herbaceous and ornamental collections, had been staffed almost entirely by women during the war. In the 'Arboretum Records (1891–1925 & 1941)' in Kew's archives a note in the section for July 1916 records that two women had started work in the Arboretum, the first to do so as so many men had left and despite the work being seen as too 'laborious' for women. 'The department is feeling acutely the shortage of labour,' it notes, and maintenance became the order of the day. Work at this time is listed as 'mowing, watering, weeding, clearing up fallen limbs, some planting and some felling'. Joining such a male-dominated team in the Arboretum must have been intimidating for these women but they were clearly determined.

SPRING

Although the 'Arboretum Records' does not note the names of the women who pioneered this role in arboriculture at Kew, Lucy H Joshua's reminiscences published later by the Kew Guild record that Miss Anna Belle Freda and Miss Nellie Robshaw – who both came from Chesham Gardens in Manchester – worked in the Arboretum and its nursery in 1916 and 1917. Here, they worked under Arboretum Foreman Arthur Osborn and would have had responsibilities for growing and caring for a wide range of rare and beautiful trees. In the staff photo of women gardeners taken in November 1916, Anna Belle and Nellie sit together on the front row next to Lucy, all smiling in their best coats and hats. In her staff file in Kew's archives is a letter from Nellie to William Watson that expresses dismay at being asked to move from her 'interesting and beloved work' in the Arboretum to the 'dismal' Ferneries section. She describes how happy she has been and how she wants to see the young trees she's grown be planted out in the Gardens.

By 1918, Nellie had moved to become a sub-foreman in the Herbaceous department, but by 1920 most women, including Nellie and Anna Belle, are recorded as having left, as men returned from the war. What their exact roles had been in the Arboretum is not known but based on their extensive previous experience of working outdoors, their contribution was surely significant. It came at the same time as the setting up of the Women's Forestry Service (WFS), part of the Women's Land Army. As historian Mark Johnston – who formerly completed a work placement at Kew – has noted, by 1918, 400 women were employed in forestry in Britain, and women's contribution to arboriculture had unquestionably begun.

It was only at the advent of the Second World War, however, that such positions were once again available to women at Kew. Fourteen women gardeners arrived in 1940, with a further thirteen in 1941. This was noted in the *Kew Guild Journal*, which described how women were now 'part of the Kew landscape'. The 1941 edition notes that a lecture was given on 'the future of women in horticulture' by the curator on 7 January, but also that three lectures were given by women that year to the student gardeners, an occurrence that was to continue. By 1946, 31 women were employed in the Gardens, but, sadly, their exact roles are not recorded, and it is telling that no women who worked in the Gardens are included in the official staff lists, being considered as either students or temporary. As with the First World War, many thousands of women joined the Women's Timber Corps (the renamed WFS) and became Lumberjills, and women were certainly employed as such at

Kew's sister garden at Bedgebury Pinetum – set up and run by Kew's William Dallimore. Today, while women remain in the minority in arboriculture, Kew – and particularly Cecily – are contributing to changing the status quo. When Kew Gardens hosted the first Women in Arboriculture networking day in 2023, it was attended by over 100 tree-care professionals, the majority of them women. Cecily was, of course, on hand to give them a tour of the Arboretum.

Today, the Tree Gang's routine work caring for the Arboretum is a very egalitarian affair, with all the arborists, irrespective of their gender, stepping in to fulfil whatever roles are required. The bulk of this work involves caring for the trees in a way that both optimizes their health and keeps people safe, be they members of the public, Kew staff or contractors. This involves a wide array of tasks, including pruning and deadwooding; felling trees, such as the diseased beech; removing old stumps; using 'air spade' tools to aerate the soil; mulching; and planting new saplings. 'Every morning when we start the day, we have a chat about what we are going to do,' explains supervisor Tom. 'I don't tend to plan masses of work beforehand because so many factors could ruin the timetable – such as a fallen branch needing immediate attention – so we just plan jobs that need to be done before the Gardens open at 10am. Aside from that we open up our computerized system and see what needs to be done and which parts of the Gardens are likely to be less busy.'

The system Tom refers to is a piece of software called 'Tree Smart' developed by the company Kaarbon Tech. It is essentially a stand-alone, map-based tree-assessment program, which currently has information on all specimens in the Arboretum that have known GPS latitude and longitude coordinates – 8,358 trees in total. Eventually, the hope is to have all the trees recorded in this way. The digital map at the system's heart divides the Gardens into three zones. Zone 1 encompasses trees around the perimeter that could present a round-the-clock risk to people, as they could drop a limb or fall outside the Gardens' walls. Zone 2 comprises trees across the bulk of the site, which, if not in good health, could potentially harm visitors or workers within the walls during working hours. And Zone 3 comprises the Natural Area, which, having limited public access, is considered a lower-risk area. Trees in Zone 1 are inspected at least once a year; those in Zone 2, at least once every three years; and those in Zone 3, every three to five years.

Tom uses Tree Smart to work out what work needs doing

when, which includes allocating work flagged up by earlier assessments and planning new inspections. As he fires up the system on the desktop computer in his office in the former stable block that serves as the Tree Gang's workshop, the digital map of Kew shows red paths criss-crossing sections of green and encircling the major buildings and water features. Then, as he zooms in, individual trees appear on the green areas as circles. To plan work for the Gang, Tom can ask a general question of the system, such as 'What work is currently flagged as due for completion before the end of the month?'. Or he can pose a more specific query such as: 'What trees are currently considered high risk?' (there shouldn't be any, he quickly confirms); 'When was tree X planted?'; or 'Which trees need deadwooding?'. The answers to such questions form the basis of a 'work package' of information that can be downloaded onto a tablet version of Tree Smart and taken into the Gardens. Usefully, this app automatically includes data on neighbouring specimens too, so if the Gang spot a tree in need of attention close to where they are working, they can immediately make a note of it on the system. Likewise, once a work task has been completed, the team can update the tablet in the field.

Tom usually undertakes the tree assessments himself,

a task for which he draws experience from his first job as a utility arborist clearing vegetation around power lines. That role taught him to be disciplined, and to appreciate the need for robust health and safety standards. Tom's love for trees, meanwhile, had been instilled during his childhood, when he spent much time exploring around a pre-Roman path known as Ladies Walk, near where he grew up in Andover, Hampshire. In 1863, the trail had been planted with 121 trees to commemorate the wedding of the Prince of Wales (later King Edward VII) to Princess Alexandra of Denmark, which provided an array of horse chestnuts, beech, oak and sycamore for young Tom and his friends to climb. 'I've always liked oaks; one of the trees in the area that we used to climb in was called the Crazy Tree. It was a huge tree with huge horizontal limbs. If my mum came and saw us doing these sorts of things, I would not be allowed to go up there.'

In 2007, aged 16, Tom went to Sparsholt College, Winchester, where he first studied Wildlife and Countryside Management and then, the following year, undertook a National Certificate in Arboriculture. This led to his utility arborist role, after which he spent five years working for a small family company providing tree care on large estates and in formal gardens. The role allowed Tom to finesse his arboricultural skills and paved the way for him to join Kew as a climbing arborist in 2017. After joining the Gardens, he took the opportunity to study for his Level 4 Diploma in Arboriculture at Merrist Wood College and was promoted to Arboricultural Supervisor.

In his current job, Tom carries out tree assessments in the Gardens two or three times a week. These inspections are planned in a similar way to other work, for example by asking Tree Smart to highlight all trees that are due for an assessment within a particular timeframe. Tom can then look at where those trees are on the map, plan a set of trees to inspect and his route between them, and then download the appropriate work package. Once Tom is in the Gardens, ready to start an assessment, the Tree Smart software guides him to answer questions as he observes a particular tree. These are based on a methodology developed by the International Society of Arboriculture (ISA) which also underpins the ISA's Tree Risk Assessment Qualification. They guide the assessor to first consider factors relating to how frequently the site around the tree is occupied by people, and the characteristics of the site itself, such as the topography, soil conditions, prevailing wind and any history of ground failure. From there, the app directs the user to begin looking closely at the tree itself.

Today, managing an Arboretum is a far more high-tech operation than in the past.

Examining a young, short tree with a small-diameter trunk in the heart of the Arboretum might only take Tom a few minutes. But assessing a very old, large tree with lots of features could take him an hour or more. It might involve probing the trunk or hitting it gently with a sounding mallet to ensure it is not rotten or hollow, using binoculars to look carefully at the unions of trunk and branches to identify any potential weaknesses, and peering up through the crown to see how much sky is visible and whether the canopy looks dense and healthy. If the crown of a usually leafy tree has begun to look sparse and thin, it might be because it has succumbed to a disease like ash dieback or because its leaves are being eaten by hungry oak processionary moth caterpillars. Ultimately, through a careful assessment of the potential visitors, the surrounds, the tree and any notes from previous assessments, rankings for the likelihood of failure and any potential consequences are determined. These help to identify mitigating actions to be taken, which then informs the future work packages for the Tree Gang.

If an assessment reveals signs that a tree is not as healthy as it should be but does not pose an immediate risk, Tom increases the frequency of the inspections. When a regular triennial assessment had revealed that brittle cinder fungus had invaded the recently felled beech, Tom had begun scheduling six-monthly assessments. In that case, as the brittle cinder fungus had invaded the tensile side of the tree, affecting its stability and ability to hold itself up, the decision had been taken to remove it well before it might fail. Sometimes, however, it can be possible to prolong the life of a diseased tree by initially cutting back the canopy to shrink the leaf area it has to maintain; limiting the potential for wind damage and reducing structural load by shortening or removing branches; or by using an air spade to make the soil around its roots less compact, so it can access water and nutrients more easily.

Understanding how far a destructive fungus has advanced is key to knowing the best course of action. For this the Tree Gang sometimes use a tool called 'sonic tomography'. This works in a similar way to using a sounding mallet – where the assessor seeks to 'hear' from the tap of the hammer if the wood is hollow – but involves more sophisticated technology that enables the user to visualize the inside of the tree.

Using the tool involves placing 12 sensors into the bark at even distances around a trunk and attaching them to a laptop. Each sensor is then tapped, in turn, with a hammer.

This sends sound waves through the wood to be received by the other sensors. Dedicated software analyses the velocity at which these waves are detected to determine the density of the timber. Wave velocities are then plotted on a digital cross-section of the tree called a tomogram, with different colours used to represent fast-, medium- or slow-wave velocities. Fast velocities are desirable as these depict healthy wood; slower speeds can indicate defects, such as decay, cracks or cavities. The process can be repeated at different heights to build up a three-dimensional model of the internal state of the trunk – a little like a human MRI scan – which can then be used to determine the strength and safety of the tree. The technology is particularly helpful for managing important living collections of trees, such as Kew's Arboretum, as it means that diseased trees can be helped to live for as long as possible.

While caring for Kew's unique living collection of trees forms a large proportion of the Tree Gang's work, there are sometimes opportunities for them to do something out of the ordinary and share their work with others. One such opportunity arises when CBBC's iconic *Blue Peter* programme comes to visit. Their aim is for 42nd presenter Abby Cook to become an honorary member of the Gang for the day and get her Blue Peter green badge for helping the environment. Aided by the whole team, Abby is helped into a harness, securely roped up, and then winched up into a towering London plane tree (*Platanus* x *hispanica*) near the Palm House to help measure its height, assess its health and remove some dead wood. Being terrified of heights, she does not find it an easy assignment. Tom and Rich, who accompany her up into the tree, provide a calming influence. From a limb high in the uppermost branches, Tom explains that measuring the trees at Kew gives the team a good idea of how well they are growing and their overall health.

Tom reaches up from where he is balancing to the top of the uppermost branches with a bamboo pole that he knows is 2.5 metres long and attaches a measuring tape to the bottom, which Abby then drops to the ground and the crew below. They judge the tree to be around 31.5 metres tall. Tom looks as if he belongs in the treetops, perfectly balancing his weight on the branches and admiring the view, while Abby clings to her ropes as any person with a fear of heights would. Nonetheless, she is more than able to articulate what they are doing for the camera and why it is important. This is an inspiring encounter for the presenter, the Tree Gang and the young viewers alike, and an invaluable opportunity to encourage children to see the many different career options of working with trees. For Abby, who has a condition called Ehlers-Danlos Syndrome (EDS), and often has to use a wheelchair to get about, it's also a chance to show that disability is not a barrier, especially in your love of nature.

The euphoria of Abby's successful climb has hardly receded when the Tree Gang receive word of a threat that needs their rapid attention. Eggs of the oak processionary moth (*Thaumetopoea processionea*) or OPM, raised in captivity on Hampstead Heath, in north London, have begun to hatch. This means that the same species of black-and-grey larvae are likely, too, to be emerging from egg masses, or plaques, high in the branches of Kew Gardens' oaks. If not apprehended they will undergo six moults, or 'instars', that will see them grow from 3mm to 35mm long over 12 or so weeks, shedding skin as the available food increases and the temperature creeps up. Initially bald, after their third moult, at 10–15mm long, they will begin producing toxic silvery hairs and moving en masse in furry nose-to-tail cavalcades along branches and down trunks, munching their way through the fresh leaves of the new season. And by the fourth instar, they will be building pale-coloured tents, which can each contain as many as 700,000 hairs from shed skin. Left to their own devices, they will, by late September, have pupated into moths that will lay eggs and generate another year of caterpillars the following spring. While Kew seeks to preserve biodiversity, this voracious and toxic creature presents a risk to both its precious oak collection and the many visitors who come to wander in and admire the Arboretum in summer.

A notifiable pest, the caterpillar's hairs can harm people and animals, causing itchy skin rashes and breathing difficulties, irritating eyes and throat, and prompting allergic reactions. With the risk highest when the caterpillars are most active, Kew seeks to prevent the larvae from undergoing their third moult, by spraying the oak leaves just when the caterpillars are hungry and starting to feed. The treatment contains the dead bacteria *Bacillus thuringiensis*. When the caterpillars eat the bacteria-coated oak leaves, they then stop eating and die before pupating. The timing is critical; not only does the caterpillar need to be in its hungriest developmental stage, the weather must also be clement, as rain and wind can both reduce the bacterial-rich residue captured on the leaves. Moreover, the Tree Gang must spray around 500 of Kew's 1,400 oaks that are most at risk of infection in the early morning before visitors begin entering the Gardens.

Oak processionary moths have been resident in Kew Gardens since 2006, so it's a well-researched and rehearsed routine. The moths first arrived in the UK from the Netherlands on a consignment of cypress oaks (*Quercus robur* 'Fastigiata Koster') that were bound for two new London housing estates; one in Ealing and the other a mile or so from Kew Gardens. The Kew development had been built next to a sewage treatment plant, and the imported columnar oaks were to screen the houses from these works. No sooner had the residents moved in, however, than some began to complain of breathing problems and irritation to their eyes. Concerned that their waste-processing neighbours might be giving off harmful fumes, they called in Environmental Health experts. No problem was found with the sewage plant, but the experts did observe some unusual-looking caterpillars in the oak trees. They requested the help of entomologists at Kew Gardens, who spotted that the caterpillars were those of the oak processionary moth. Until now it had only been known to have spread north and west in mainland Europe from its Mediterranean homeland. Action was taken to suck nests from the trees with heavy-duty hoovers, but a few of the caterpillars pupated into moths. Soon, they had moved into their own dream home: the precious living collection of oaks in Kew's Arboretum.

The Tree Gang's first inkling that they had a new invasive insect in their midst was when they were called to remove a nest of caterpillars from a large oak tree close to what is now the Botanical Restaurant beside the Palm House Pond. At first, they attempted to simply remove the nest by hand, wearing rubber gloves and face masks to protect themselves. But they soon realized that the larvae have a habit of firing out their fibre-glass-like hairs (of which each individual can have 62,000). A new tactic was tried, which involved spraying the nests with hair lacquer – to freeze the toxic hairs contained within them in place – before setting fire to them. 'All that happened,' explains Will 'was that the hair lacquer burned off in a flash, the nest burst open and out came hundreds of angry caterpillars firing their little poison arrows left, right and centre. Tony Kirkham [former Head of Arboretum, Gardens and Horticultural Services], who had fair skin and ginger hair, only had to walk under an infected tree and he'd start tingling. He was like our canary. But I was called the rhino hide because I never seemed to have any problems with it.'

Next, the Tree Gang tried the hoovering method of moth removal. Up they would go in a cherry picker, suited and booted and with battery-operated respirators, to suck the nests from the trees. But the moth population exploded exponentially.

Whereas in the first year there had been one nest, by the second there were ten nests, and by the next there were 80. A new approach to tackling the moths was needed. By now, a company called Bartlett Tree Experts had developed a rig that could be used to spray an insecticide targeting caterpillars, so Kew decided to try this method. The timing on when to spray was guided by a contact in the Netherlands who emailed Kew when he noticed his captive OPM eggs hatching out. However, the problem was that the third instar phase, indicated as the best time for spraying, seemed set to coincide with Kew's annual Bluebells and Broomsticks festival in early May. Historically, the Tree Gang had installed a zip line for children ahead of the popular event, at which visitors could view the annual carpet of bluebell blossom and see besom broom-making displays. But the prospect of toxic caterpillars mingling with festival-goers meant that the event had to be cancelled.

Since then, the Gardens have been sprayed annually, with the exception of 2013, when the decision was taken to see if spraying alternate years might be sufficient to control the population. It wasn't. Back the caterpillars came with a vengeance, and so the annual spring OPM spraying resumed. To start with, treating the Garden's at-risk oak trees took a full week. But the Tree Gang have now got the process down to a fine art and are able to get through the task in a matter of hours. Having the latest technology helps, which has been greatly refined since the early days of spraying. Bartlett now has two types of spraying rig at its disposal: high volume and ultra-low volume. The high-volume rig works in the manner of a pressure washer, sending a strong jet of liquid up to ten metres high, which then falls back down covering the leaves. This is good for the trees with a low canopy and for targeting tree trunks. In contrast, the ultra-low-volume or electrostatic delivery method acts like a giant fan, with the treatment being injected into a large column of rising air. With this system, the liquid is vaporised and travels high into the canopy, making it suitable for treating tall trees.

This year, the spraying date has been set for 24 May. The Gardens have been divided into four clover-leaf-shaped sections, and a team made up of two Bartlett staff and two Tree Gang members have been allocated to tackling the oaks within each section. To speed up the process, the Tree Gang have already put yellow-and-black plastic tape on the trees that are to be sprayed. These comprise all trees of species known to be favoured by the moth, mainly European and some American species, plus any individual specimens highlighted by the Tree Smart system as having been infested in the past.

Around 40 to 50 species will be treated in total. At 5.30am, the teams set off in their different directions from the Tree Gang's workshop, keen to make the most of the day. The Bartlett staff, who will be doing the spraying, are mostly dressed in blue protective suits with luminous yellow helmets, while the Kew team sport white boiler suits and masks to protect them from the spray.

By 8.45am most of the demarcated trees have been sprayed, with just a couple of American oaks remaining on the Pagoda Vista close to the Pavilion café. This is a job for Tom and Rich's team, who are working with Bartlett's Dean Jones and Aidan Neill with a high-volume rig. Luckily, the conditions have remained perfect for spraying all morning, with the air still and the blue sky largely clear of clouds. As Dean directs the jet of insecticide up into the foliage of the last tree of the morning, the sunlight generates a momentary rainbow, before the moisture falls back down to coat the leaves.

With the voracious eating of the caterpillars now, hopefully, curtailed for this year, all that remains is for the spraying teams to enjoy a hearty arborist's breakfast. Back at the Tree Gang's workshop, the Bartlett team, their boiler suits now shed like spent larvae skins to reveal luminous yellow and dark green company T-shirts, have set up a large hotplate powered by a red gas canister on the central bench in the main workroom. The day's designated chef, Bartlett's Arborist Representative Tom Adamson, piles the hotplate high with hash browns and bacon, before breaking eggs into the remaining spaces. Each one sizzles and splutters as the egg white bubbles in the heat. Beside the hotplate sits a large steaming saucepan of beans, while in the adjoining kitchen, sausages, mushrooms and rolls are being prepared. The smell of coffee and the sound of laughter mingle, as everyone grabs a plate and cutlery, and queues up for food. Soon they are all tucking into a large fry-up, happy that the intensive moth-eradicating routine is over for another year. Having had such an early start, the Tree Gang's working day is over by 10am – just as visitors start to arrive.

While the spraying is anticipated to take place again at Kew in the coming years, there is the possibility that one day the moths might be controlled by a natural predator that may already be hot on their trail. Writing in an article in the summer 2024 issue of *The ARB Magazine*, the quarterly publication for members of the Arboricultural Association, Alasdair Nicoll, Senior Arborist for Hampstead Heath, related recent observations of oak processionary moth numbers across the 3,000 to 4,000 oaks on Hampstead Heath, and in

Highgate Wood and Queens Park, London. He noted that while the number of nests in these oaks grew from 15 in 2015 to nearly 200 in 2017 and 2,000 in 2018, in 2019 the numbers dropped off to 1,000 and since then have fallen further, appearing to stabilize at 300 to 400 annually in subsequent years. He considered that two natural predators of the moth could be the cause, namely great tits (*Parus major*) and the large black fly (*Carcelia iliaca*).

Nicoll reported that great tits had been observed eating oak processionary moth caterpillars in significant numbers in continental Europe and, from 2017, had also been spotted doing so on Hampstead Heath. The following year, the presence of *C. iliaca* had also been confirmed on the Heath. This fly is a parasitoid, the larvae of which like to live in oak processionary moth caterpillars and eat them from the inside. An experiment conducted on the Heath indicated that the average percentages of caterpillars parasitized by *Carcelia* between 2019 and 2022 ranged from 60 per cent to more than 80 per cent. Other predators of the oak processionary moth had also been spotted in the locale, including another tachinid fly, *Pales processioneae* (which is the most significant parasitoid of oak processionary moth on the continent) and two species of ichneumon wasps. Nicoll concluded by writing: 'Although [oak processionary moth] has been introduced to the UK and has never been native here, in time the moths will become part of the UK ecosystem, along with the things that eat them. Perhaps it is time we shifted the focus of our strategy towards living with them.'

Being able to manage OPM 'naturally' at Kew, while still maintaining visitor safety, would be greatly welcomed. A study of oaks growing wild in the UK found that the native sessile oak (*Quercus petraea*) and the English oak (*Q. robur*) support over 2,300 other species, including invertebrates, birds, mammals, lichen and fungi. The oaks at Kew, too, have the potential to support diverse species, and, while the insecticide Kew currently uses to tackle OPM is the least damaging spray available – and does not harm the trees themselves – it is known to be toxic to some other insects, including other butterflies and moths. With Kew's mission being to understand and protect plants and fungi for the well-being of people and the future of all life on Earth – and its oak and other living collections vital for helping it do so – it has a fine line to tread.

The oak collection at Kew is one of the most extensive in the country, encompassing 149 oak taxa (species, subspecies and hybrids) not to mention numerous cultivars (produced by selective breeding). It includes many notable, historic and rare individuals grown from wild-collected seed – many from the USA, China, Japan, Europe and the Near East, as well as Palestine, Vietnam and Bhutan. Kew's collection is thought to be one of the oldest and most diverse oak collections in the world. Its oldest specimens date from when the royals landscaped the area in the 18th century and has been built up as a taxonomic collection since the mid-19th century. At a time when oaks are in decline around the world, due to a variety of pests, pathogens and climate change, it is an unrivalled scientific resource.

The majority of oaks reside alongside Riverside Walk, with the main collection stretching from Brentford Gate to the end of Syon Vista parallel to the Thames towpath. But there are oaks dotted all over the Gardens. From the enormous, domed chestnut-leaved oaks near the Orangery and Waterlily House in the north, past American pin oaks under the Treetop Walkway, and Asian sawtooth oaks near Victoria Gate, to plentiful English oaks in the Conservation Area around Queen Charlotte's Cottage in the south, they all add their majestic beauty to the landscape. The variety of leaves, acorns and overall forms of oaks is quite extraordinary. 'When I first came to Kew I thought I knew trees but I was just blown away with how many different oaks there are here,' admits Tom. 'Around the world, there are over 500 different species of oak ranging from the tropics, from Cambodia, right through America, Mexico, Europe and Russia – the variety in that genus is just insane.'

Many of Kew's specimens are original introductions to Britain (in other words, the first ones to come into the country) and are of enormous scientific and horticultural value. One such is Kew's largest oak and indeed largest tree by volume in the Gardens. This is the immense chestnut-leaved oak (*Quercus castaneifolia*) near the Waterlily House, which stands 37 metres tall and has a trunk girth of 8 metres. These statistics have earned it the accolade of Champion Tree for its species, and a place in the Tree Register of the British Isles, which records exceptional specimens of tree species, and the largest and tallest trees in Britain and Ireland. This species was scientifically described in 1831, by German botanist and explorer Carl Anton von Meyer, who then introduced its seed to Britain in 1843. Kew's tree was grown from this first batch of seed and planted out in the Gardens in 1846. This tree has stood through almost 180 years of storms and droughts, with plenty of visitors coming to stand under its boughs.

In fact, the tree's immense size has drawn so many people that it has had to be fenced off to prevent the compaction of the soil around its roots. In recent years the Tree Gang have used their expertise to boost the health of the soil around this tree and de-compact the soil.

Other oaks not far away from this giant treasure have also become significant to the history of Kew and horticulture, including the Lucombe oak (*Q.* x *hispanica* 'Lucombeana') on Syon Vista. This is remembered as the tree that had to be moved – as an already mature specimen – to make way for the new Syon Vista, which stretches out from the back of the Palm House to the River Thames and a view of Syon House across the water. The Lucombe oak is a true heritage tree embodying elements of the history of this landscape and the people who worked here. Originally raised by nurseryman William Lucombe in 1762, it was gifted to Kew in 1773 and grew to be a fine tree. However, in 1846, Director William Hooker and his landscape designer William Nesfield needed to move it. With much labour, it is thought that a trench was dug between the tree and its final position some 20 metres away. It was then dragged by oxen just to the side of the main avenue where soil was mounded up around its roots.

Remarkably, it survived this treatment, and it still stands proudly on its mound today and has become one of Kew's most characterful trees.

There are many beautiful and unusual oaks to find at Kew including the golden oak (*Q. alnifolia*) from Cyprus, which has bright yellow undersides to its leaves, the threatened *Q. insignis* from Mexico, which produces the largest acorns in the world, the northern pin oak (*Q. ellipsoidalis*) from the prairies of North America, the pointed leaves of which turn an exceptional scarlet in autumn, and even *Q.* x *kewensis*, a hybrid raised in the Gardens in 1914. Often there are several specimens of the same species, each from different wild locations or even from other gardens or nurseries. This ensures that a range of genetic diversity is represented in that species (in the same way that a crowd of people will contain wide-ranging genes, giving individuals different appearances and traits). As oak seeds – acorns – are 'recalcitrant' and cannot be dried and stored in a seed bank, species or special individuals must be either grown-on straight away and kept as a living library, or the acorns must be cryopreserved at ultra-low temperatures. However, the latter is costly and still not reliable as a method. Kew's Arboretum has therefore become an important genetic repository for oak species for future scientific research and conservation, as well as a wonderful place to marvel at the sheer diversity of just one genus of tree.

As spring moves towards early summer across the Arboretum, species gathered from across the temperate world begin to flower – from the delicate white flowers of the Japanese snowbell (*Styrax japonicus*) to the large fragrant blooms of the California buckeye (*Aesculus californica*). Sap is rising in all the trees, bringing new life and colour to the Gardens. Trees are responding to the changes in day length, temperature and rainfall as the season evolves. Wildflowers, bulbs such as the blue *Camassia*, and a wealth of grasses are also now growing and flowering before the leaf canopy above becomes too dark, forming an important understorey layer that benefits the resident biodiversity, and helps to cool the soil and air temperature among the trees.

After the buds break and new leaves unfurl towards the spring sun, trees can start to make food (glucose and carbohydrates) through the process of photosynthesis. This remarkable chemical process, driven by sunlight, shapes the growth cycle of the tree. Primary growth results in new stems, leaves and flowers, while secondary growth in the thin layer of vascular cambium tissue under the bark enables a tree to put on new wood and increase in girth. The tree uses vessels called xylem to distribute water and nutrients from the roots upwards to the leaves and uses phloem vessels to carry sugars from its leafy extremities downwards through the tree and to its roots. The enormous amount of activity inside the trunk of a tree as water rushes up to the canopy can even be heard as loud rumbles, pops and whistles, as demonstrated by artist Alex Metcalf using highly sensitive microphones in his Tree Listening Project, which he has demonstrated at Kew. Throughout spring and into summer, trees are incredibly dynamic beings.

Understanding how trees respond to and regulate temperature and moisture in the environment is becoming an important focus for arboricultural research. This is one of the strands of work that Tree Gang member Kevin Martin is involved with in his position as Head of Tree Collections at the Gardens. Overall, Kevin's role is to curate and manage Kew's trees and shrubs for scientific research and conservation within the Gardens' historic landscape. This involves conducting surveys on the potential impacts of events or new building works in the Gardens to ensure that no trees are damaged; attending conferences to share Kew's knowledge and experiences; journeying abroad to gather new seeds and other materials; meeting potential philanthropists who are minded to financially support Kew's Arboretum; talking all things trees with the media; and, in his spare time, studying for a research degree.

As part of this role, Kevin is currently involved in a collaborative scientific project to better understand temperature and moisture in the 'microclimates' around trees in the Gardens. This research is under way at five national sites including here in the Arboretum. The goal is to understand how microclimates affect pest and disease outbreaks, to help with monitoring and planning for biosecurity risks. In this context, the term microclimate can refer to the small-scale climate of a specific area such as the Gardens or even very small distinct parts of Kew. The variability of planting and different types of leaf canopy in the Gardens offers a good variety of microclimates, as is evident by walking from the warmer, windier open spaces to the much cooler, shadier parts of the Pinetum, for example.

It seems remarkable that monitoring such variables in microclimates around individual trees can translate into modelling predictions about pest and disease outbreaks, but such pests and pathogens are proven to respond to changes in the microclimates where they live. To more accurately forecast when and where outbreaks might occur, researchers at the University of Exeter have created a model estimating temperature and humidity in different habitats. Kevin is working to help verify this model by measuring temperatures around individual trees – under their canopy, inside their trunks and below the soil. The results show how widely measurements can vary around one individual tree but also how much they differ from the official Meteorological Office weather station at Kew, which is positioned on a wide expanse of open lawn close to the Orangery. Being involved in this work means that Kew will be at the forefront of understanding and tackling its own pest and disease problems.

Oak processionary moths are not the only invaders of concern; increasing numbers of pests and diseases are reaching our shores. According to the Woodland Trust, 16 new pests and diseases have arrived in the UK since the year 2000, and some of these are proving very serious indeed. These include fungal and bacterial diseases and viruses, as well as a whole range of new insect pests.

Ash dieback (caused by the fungus *Hymenoscyphus fraxineus*) for example, is predicted to destroy over 80 per cent of Britain's ash trees, changing our treescapes forever just as Dutch Elm Disease (from the fungus *Ophiostoma novo-ulmi*) did from the 1960s. *Phytophthora ramorum* – the name literally means plant destroyer – is an oomycete (a fungus-like organism) best known for causing potato blight. It is now a real threat to certain trees. Thousands of larch trees have already been lost across Britain to this disease, and it has the potential to spread to other species. Forest Research has gone so far as to enrol the work of a sniffer dog called Ivor from Canine Assisted Pest Eradication to monitor the deadly disease. So far, the results look promising, with the six-year-old cocker spaniel Labrador cross detecting the pathogen in 89 per cent of tests. Meanwhile needle blights, including *Dothistroma septosporum* and *Diplodia sapinea* are causing huge problems in conifers across the UK, including at Kew, turning their needles brown and preventing them from photosynthesizing.

New insects, including horse chestnut leaf miner (*Cameraria ohridella*), are also already causing noticeable damage, while others such as emerald ash borer (*Agrilus planipennis*) and red-necked longhorn beetle (*Aromia bungii*) are on the watch list. If they arrive in the UK, they could cause untold damage to our woodlands, forestry and gardens. At Kew, the loss to carefully curated collections could be devastating. This new research will deliver scientifically robust data, hopefully creating useful tools for those working with trees and forests across the whole of the UK. Kew is taking part in this wider experiment to reflect trees growing in city locations, to complement the other trial sites, which are in more rural settings.

Taking part in this experiment are six tall *Picea abies* 'Laxa' conifers from southern Europe that are growing near the Lake, and six English oaks. Each looks as if it is undergoing hospital treatment. Black strapping and wiring envelop and snake around the trees' bark, while bright yellow sensors have been installed into their trunks and nearby a sensor resembling a nightmarishly large syringe is measuring air temperature. 'What we're doing is measuring the thermals inside the trees,' says Kevin, 'We have thermocouples [sensors for measuring temperature] that go just under the bark about two centimetres in on the south and the north sides. We then have a thermometer on the outside.' Temperature is measured inside and outside the tree every ten minutes, as beetle outbreaks are often associated with sun-warmed stems.

Kevin is going beyond this to also use the instruments installed at Kew – together with dendrometers that measure tree growth – to better understand how the trees themselves respond to changes in the microclimates around them.

He is particularly interested in how climate change may be contributing to 'acute oak decline'. This disease, associated with several bacteria and a beetle, has been killing both English and sessile oaks in the UK for 30 years and is starting to cause problems at Kew. The disease causes the xylem inside the tree to rot, with the result that rising sap weeps out of cavities in alarming black 'bleeds'. The myriad reasons for this disease are not fully understood, although organizations like Action Oak are actively investing in research.

Kevin has a theory that acute oak decline is related to how climate change is affecting the growing season for trees. Oaks have evolved to drop their leaves in autumn – normally around October in the UK – but this has been delayed in recent years until December at Kew. Kevin thinks that there are physical consequences to this delay and that the shorter dormancy period over winter may weaken the tree. He has seen that the bleeds characteristic of this disease are starting to flow from the bark very early in the spring, meaning that the bacteria must be feeding on something already in the wood, which he conjectures are carbohydrates in the xylem vessels that haven't had time to be pulled down to the roots over the short winter period.

Trees suck up water from the ground, pass it up through their xylem and evaporate it through their leaves in a process called transpiration. The rate at which it occurs is driven by 'vapour pressure deficit' (the difference between the vapour pressure of the air when saturated and the actual vapour pressure of the air). Dendrometers strapped around the trunks of the oaks are recording how the stems swell and shrink according to the temperature and available moisture. 'When it's hot the trees shrink and when wetter and cooler they swell because they're taking up water – and they can retain it. When you get a high-vapour-pressure-deficit day, the water demand goes up, but the trees can't keep up with that demand and that's when they start to shrink. They go into a stress mode and start to look at how they retain that moisture,' reveals Kevin. This is science in action, showing exactly when the trees are active and how long for. Data over the next year will either prove or disprove Kevin's theories or may even throw up new hypotheses to test.

The contribution from the small invasion of the bark on these trees will therefore hopefully be profound for the whole Arboretum and many treescapes beyond. For now, though, these trees continue to soak up the spring sunshine and make the most of the current rainfall, as the days begin to lengthen, the air begins to warm and early summer approaches.

Part Two

SUMMER

Monday, 22 July 2024, is a busy day for Kevin. The Kew Gardens media team is releasing a new report outlining how Kew aims to keep its Arboretum thriving in the face of climate change. As Kevin has undertaken much of the research for the report, he is to be a key media contact, alongside Simon Toomer, Curator of Living Collections, and Richard Barley, Kew's Director of Gardens.[1] No sooner has the press release been sent out than all three are in demand. Kevin is interviewed by Kay Burley of Sky News, Simon Toomer speaks with *ITV Evening News*, and Richard Barley is on LBC's evening news. Media outlets around the world run news stories and features about the report. 'Is Kew Gardens heading for TREEMAGEDDON?' asks the *Daily Mail*. 'Climate threat spurs London's Kew Gardens to look for resilient trees', explains Reuters. Even the *Macao News* warns

---

1 Raoul Curtis-Machin from RBG Edinburgh replaced Richard Barley as the Director of Gardens in summer 2025. Alex Summers from Cambridge University Botanic Garden took over from Simon Toomer as Curator of Living Collections, also in summer 2025.

its readers that 'London's iconic botanic garden is at risk from climate change'.

The media frenzy is a response to the report's main message: with London's climate in 2050 set to be akin to that of Barcelona, Spain, today, as many as half of Kew's 11,000 trees could be really struggling by 2090. But it is not all bad news. The report lays out a series of actions that Kew plans to take to ensure the Arboretum remains intact and healthy under future conditions. These include: selecting species that are adapted to the forecast climatic conditions; increasing diversity by incorporating trees of different ages, species and provenances; moving away from taxonomic planting, where trees from a single family or genus are grouped together, towards arranging plants to satisfy environmental and landscape requirements; and clustering plants that need high or low levels of water so that, where required, watering can be carried out as efficiently as possible. It is the first report of its kind produced by a botanic garden in the UK.

The need for Kew to plan for a warmer future had slowly become more apparent. Kew's Living Collections Strategy (2019), acknowledged 'that climate change may present a challenge for some taxa within the outdoor living collections at Kew'. And the World Heritage Site Management Plan

2020–2025, written as the Covid-19 pandemic was presenting a more immediate concern to major attractions around the globe, noted that decisions around the planting of long-lived taxa within the landscape need to consider 'the suitability of each taxon for the likely future growing conditions'. But it was the UK drought of 2022 that brought the reality of climate change sharply into focus. The summer was among the hottest and driest since records began, and the first year in which the UK had recorded a temperature of 40°C. More than 450 trees died at Kew; a loss second only to the Great Storm of 1986 in its devastating impact on the Arboretum. With trees having the potential to live for hundreds of years, a strategic plan was needed to ensure the Arboretum would endure in the uncertain climate of years to come.

Towering above the Waterlily House, west of the Broad Walk, is the Gardens' Champion chestnut-leaved oak. The oak was planted in 1846, three years after seeds were first brought into Britain by Carl Anton von Meyer, from the tree's native region of the Caucasus mountains and northern Iran. In the wild, the oak favours north-facing slopes, where, between sea level and 2,100 metres' (6890 feet) altitude it forms humid forests, and above which it appears as scattered specimens. This oak is an unusual sight in Britain as this species is rarely planted here. In spring, Kew's majestic specimen had unfurled bronze-tinted, long, serrated leaves that had turned a deep glossy green as the days warmed, forming a spectacular 3,000-square-metre crown. Far from looking scorched and unhappy as the temperature at Kew pushes up to 32°C at the end of July – a record for the year so far – the tree looks in rude health.

When he had started work at Kew in May 2012, Kevin had been set on climbing this tree; it was the biggest, after all, and he had been a competitive climber in his past. Despite his experience, Kevin found his first ascent of the oak quite daunting. He had not climbed a tree that big before and it wasn't possible to get his hands around the trunk as it was simply too wide. It was in the days, too, when the Tree Gang were still using the more physically demanding moving rope technique. And because the ropes used at Kew at the time were only 37 metres long in contrast to the 60-metre ones employed today, it was necessary to create a 'first stage'. This meant that all the arborists had to use the same rope to access the tree, only then attaching themselves to their individual climbing lines. It took five days for the team to deadwood the oak in Kevin's first year. It was hard work but presented him with the opportunity to study it. The tree soon became his firm favourite, and he wanted to know more about why the oak was so big and successful. 'I was interested in the tree's structure and biomechanics, and to know how the tree had grown that big but was able to maintain itself,' he recalls.

Kevin had always loved trees. Having watched his tree-surgeon father working from his early years, he had known by the age of seven or eight that he wanted to follow suit. At 16, he took a Diploma in Forestry at Sparsholt College in Winchester, followed by a National Certificate in Arboriculture a year later (equivalent to today's Level 3 certificate). For the next decade, Kevin put his qualifications to good use working as a commercial tree surgeon, but when the banking crash of 2008 hit, spending on tree care dried up and work became scarce. By chance, his wife Laura saw an advert for the role of Team Leader for arboriculture at Kew and persuaded him to apply. 'I'd never written a job application or attended an interview before,' he admits, 'because in commercial arboriculture, you just turn up with your kit on, work for a day and if you're good enough you get the job.'

Kevin clearly impressed the then Head of Arboretum, Gardens and Horticultural Services, Tony Kirkham, however, as he was offered the role, and within six months was promoted to become the youngest ever Manager of Arboriculture at just 27. To shore up his qualifications, Tony sent Kevin to Merrist Wood College to gain his Level 4 qualification in Arboriculture. He enjoyed the course and decided to undertake the foundation degree in Arboriculture and Tree Management run by University Centre Myerscough and the University of Central Lancashire. As a full-time member of the Tree Gang, this involved learning online in his spare time over four years, graduating in 2019. Then, when Tony retired in 2021, Kevin took on the role of Head of Tree Collections. The following year, when the 2022 drought began culling formerly healthy trees at Kew, Kevin decided that it was time to embark on more research by taking a master's degree in plant science at Lancaster University.

Kevin grew increasingly interested in why some tree specimens – such as Kew's Champion oak – had been able to thrive during the drought, while so many others had failed. He began to search through books, papers and other reference materials in Kew's extensive library and on the internet. Among the resources he consulted was William Jackson Bean's *Trees and Shrubs Hardy in the British Isles*, the first edition of which was published in 1914, shortly after the start of the First World War. In his time, Bean, like Kevin, had been in charge of trees in the Gardens and had recorded valuable information about the provenance of the specimens he had worked with. Thanks to Bean's work and other information sources Kevin learned of the chestnut-leaved oak's natural ecosystem and the species it grew alongside in the wild – such as the Persian ironwood *(Parrotia persica)*, the Caucasian elm *(Zelkova carpinifolia)* and the Crimean lime *(Tilia dasystyla)*. He figured that being grown from seeds from a hotter, drier part of the world, such as the Caucasus, might be the reason for the oak's success.

While Kevin was deciding what research to focus on for his degree, Botanic Gardens Conservation International (BGCI) launched a new tool designed to show the likely suitability of plants to the predicted future climate scenarios of a particular location. It gave Kevin the idea of trying to assess the suitability of lime *(Tilia)* trees growing at Kew. Not only did the Gardens have an almost complete collection of the genus but limes also happened to be the most frequently used street trees in Europe, so the work could have implications for urban landscaping in the future. 'I've always liked limes and they're very well adapted here at Kew,' says Kevin. 'Out of all our trees, they're probably one of the most successful, along with oak.'

Many of Kew's lime (or linden) trees can be found between the Victoria Gate and the Marianne North Gallery, with several tucked away in the quiet glades of the Berberis Dell. Visitors entering the Gardens and heading off to the more popular areas around the Palm House might miss them altogether, but these trees are worth seeking out. Kew has approximately 288 specimens of *Tilia* – composed of 24 species, a few natural hybrids and around 20 varieties and cultivars. Considering there are only around 30 known species of *Tilia*, from across Europe, Asia and eastern North America, this is an excellent collection.

In summer, the trees' fresh, green, heart-shaped asymmetrical leaves flutter easily in the breeze. Some, such as Oliver's lime (*T. oliveri*) and the silver lime (*T. tomentosa*) have pale undersides to their leaves so when they dance in the air, flipping between green and silver, they create a stunning three-dimensional spectacle of movement. Silver limes are a popular street tree and are often planted in urban areas as they have good drought tolerance and pest resistance. Their tiny pale green flowers, which open in mid-July, release a powerful scent that attracts bees, and for many years they have been planted as a food source for honeybees across Europe. However, dead bumblebees had been noted underneath silver limes, and it had long been speculated that these had been killed by a toxin in either the nectar or the pollen. But in 2017, Kew scientists Professor Phil Stevenson and Dr Hauke Koch worked to discover that the powerful allure of the green flower was actually fooling the bumblebees, pulling them back again and again to the flowers, which, by the end of their flowering period, were providing relatively little nectar. Bees, especially bumblebees, were, in the absence of other food sources nearby, actually starving rather than being poisoned. The scientists suggested that caffeine in the nectar could be contributing to the problem, as it had also been shown to help bees remember and be loyal to a food source. They suggested that other food plants for bees should always be provided around silver limes, especially in urban areas, as bees can recover if they can access other nectar quickly. Thankfully, at Kew, there is plenty of other nectar around for these and many other species of bee.

Across Kew, one of the main areas of scientific research is trying to understand how plants have adapted to different climates and environments. What is it, for example, that enables some plants to survive in a hostile dry environment while others thrive in a wetland? The specific biological and chemical traits of a plant can reveal the secrets of its resilience. Studying the evolution, diversity and function of such traits is the task of several teams of specialists working under Phil in

Kew's science department. This research not only has huge implications for sustainable agriculture and forestry but also has the potential to help the Arboretum team plan for the future of the tree collections on-site at Kew as well as at its sister garden Wakehurst in West Sussex.

Plant traits can encompass everything from leaf size or thickness to overall plant height; how efficiently a plant uses or transports water; how quickly it can resprout after being defoliated; the density of its wood; or even how deep its roots can grow. These inherited traits are often responses to the environment in which the species in question has naturally grown in the wild, developed on evolutionary timescales of many millions of years. But in species with wide ranges, spanning different environmental conditions, the values for some traits observed in specimens at one end of the range may differ to those at the other end. These are known as adaptive traits, and are likely to have occurred on shorter timescales, in response to climatic shifts. The set of traits a particular plant has is underpinned by its 'genotype' – its unique set of genetic material. Knowing the traits of a species can help to predict how these plants might respond to a change in the environment in which they grow – ultimately helping us to understand which species, and genotypes, will cope better in a changing climate.

In recent years, scientists have begun investigating traits that might shed light on plants' abilities to withstand drought. Some plants have evolved waxy leaves with few stomata (pores that allow the exchange of oxygen and carbon dioxide, as well as water vapour) to retain moisture. Others have small hairy leaves in order to reduce air flow around the stomata and conserve water. Keeping the leaf surface-to-volume ratio low can be key where preserving water is concerned. Conifers have evolved specialist needle-like leaves for precisely this purpose, while the olive tree (*Olea europaea*) has 'trichomes' – like microscopic umbrellas on its leaf surface, keeping the moisture in. Many tree species from drier environments have also evolved deep root systems. The typical English oak has roots that may reach nine metres in depth, while those of the blue gum (*Eucalyptus globulus*), from south-eastern Australia, can extend 45 metres.

Kevin decided to focus his research on testing the drought tolerance of limes at Kew, noting from their planting records the locations they had originally come from. Specifically, he hoped to examine the drought tolerance of a single species – the small-leaved lime (*Tilia cordata*) – across its entire range and compare the results to a baseline dataset created using *T. cordata* 'Greenspire' specimens bought from Hillier

Nurseries. He aimed to use a test that was emerging as a potentially effective way to measure drought tolerance, which involves measuring 'leaf turgor loss point', the trait that regulates a plant's ability to maintain 'cell turgor pressure' while dehydrated. Put simply, this is the point at which leaves start to wilt when water is unavailable, which has been found to be an indicator of drought-induced tree mortality. 'Effectively it's a trait-based assessment of how a tree deals with drought,' explains Kevin.

He also hoped to test wood density, another plant trait linked to drought tolerance. Scientists have found that wood tends to be less dense in trees that have an abundant water supply, such as those growing in the world's rainforests, and more dense in those growing in arid areas. In general, research has shown that having denser wood, a smaller leaf area and deeper roots can all help a tree species to be more resilient to drought, while those species that are naturally shorter also have an advantage. Plants must continually take up water through their roots and stem tissues via their xylem. When a tree can't access adequate water there is a chance that water vapour bubbles can form in the xylem causing 'cavitation' – blocking the vessels and preventing water from getting where it needs to go. Research in Canada has shown that an ability to resist such blockages in the trembling aspen (*Populus tremuloides*) has made the species more drought resistant.

First, Kevin needed to assess the suitability of limes at Kew to the current and potential future climates. Although he had initially thought to use the BGCI tool for this task, he realized that the product was too simple for his needs, as it ranked species' suitability to grow in future climates on the basis of temperature alone. While plants clearly need water as well as a favourable temperature to thrive, the tool's makers had reasoned that botanical gardens have access to irrigation, so that the amount of water that plants receive could be controlled. However, with Kew seeking to reduce its water use, Kevin explicitly wanted to see which trees would be able to thrive in both hotter and drier conditions in the years ahead.

Outdoor plants at Kew have always had to be irrigated in some way due to the generally low rainfall of the south-east. In the 18th century, Princess Augusta had a 'water engine' (an Archimedes screw pump) designed and installed by the then famous engineer John Smeaton to pull water up from a well to feed the pond and water her physick garden and arboretum. This water engine sat near where the Palm House Pond is today but is long since lost. Today, plants are primarily irrigated at Kew using treated mains water delivered via a distribution network of underground water pipes. A state-of-the-art irrigation pump house, designed around the shape of a fallen leaf, supplies this network from a 280,000-litre water tank hidden in a mound near the Treetop Walkway. There is currently limited harvesting and use of rainfall, and no use of groundwater or water from the River Thames, which flows along the western edge of the Gardens. Although during periods of drought and hosepipe bans Kew is exempt from restrictions on water use so that it can irrigate its important scientific plant collections, it tends to prioritize young trees that have yet to develop robust root systems and those from cooler and wetter parts of the world that might struggle to tolerate hot, dry conditions. With models indicating that London's current reservoir capacity may struggle to meet the needs of its citizens under extreme climate change – let alone its plants – Kew's ambition, as outlined in its 2021 Sustainability Strategy, is to minimize the amount of water used in the Gardens in future.

There were no other tools on the market designed to assess a plant's suitability to meet future climate conditions, so for Kevin there was only one thing for it. If he was to continue with his degree, he would have to create his own model, one capable

Kew's Tree Gang, who look after all of Kew's trees, form a tight-knit, friendly team. Left to right: Jamie Slessor, Rich Church, Arthur Gregg, Will Harding, Cecily Withall and Tom Fry.

Kevin Martin, Head of Tree Collections, curates and manages Kew's trees and shrubs for scientific research and conservation.

Arboretum Nursery Supervisor Sal Demain.

Kew's Arboretum of temperate hardy tree species is home to over 11,000 specimens. These provide a natural backdrop to heritage buildings such as the Temperate House.

The beautiful European beech *(Fagus sylvatica)*, once common at Kew, is now beginning to struggle due to prolonged summer droughts caused by climate change.

Every tree felling operation is carefully controlled by health and safety measures and risk assessments. Keeping the public and the Tree Gang safe is paramount.

Brittle cinder fungus has invaded the heart of this European beech *(Fagus sylvatica)*, making it unsafe next to a public path. The Tree Gang conduct regular tree inspections to ensure trees in the Arboretum do not pose a risk to public safety.

At an 'away day' at Harcourt Arboretum (part of the University of Oxford Botanic Garden), the Tree Gang get to climb some impressively tall black pines *(Pinus nigra)* and share knowledge and techniques with other arborists.

William Dallimore was a renowned foreman of Kew's Arboretum in the late 19th and early 20th centuries. He wrote several seminal books on trees and pruning, and was an expert on conifers.

Tom Fry – who heads up the Arboricultural Unit team, otherwise known as the Tree Gang – mirrors the image of William Dallimore taken around 130 years earlier, showing the difference in the equipment needed by an arborist today.

Sawdust flies into the air as Tom works at height to carefully bring down sections of a black pine that will be weighed and measured to determine how much carbon the whole tree contains.

Will, Jamie and Cecily remove and cut up the remains of the black pine ahead of weighing its branches to measure its carbon content.

Cecily Withall is the first permanent female member of staff to have been employed as a climbing arborist at Kew since the 1980s. She took the Kew Arboricultural Apprenticeship and joined the Tree Gang after graduating from the two-year Horticulture with Plantsmanship diploma at Royal Botanic Garden Edinburgh.

Cecily works to prune a branch back to a main trunk. After reducing the branch she will make a final cut, leaving a pruning collar next to the trunk to allow the wound to heal over.

Tom and the Tree Gang use a system of climbing called the 'stationary rope technique', which is especially good for climbing tall trees.

Tom and apprentice Arthur Gregg put the finishing protective cage around a newly planted rare Polish larch *(Larix decidua* var. *polonica)* (propagated by Arboretum Nursery Supervisor Sal Demain) on Larch Walk.

of providing a more accurate indication of trees' potential to survive Kew's future conditions. He had no previous experience of building computer models but he wasn't going to let a simple thing like that deter him.

Kevin began by identifying the variables that had the most influence on a tree's well-being, namely temperature, rainfall and potential evapotranspiration (PET – the amount of water that would be evaporated and transpired by a specific plant or ecosystem if there was sufficient water available). His starting point for gathering this data was an existing database called TreeGoer (created by ecologist Roeland Kindt of the Kenya-based research institute World Agroforestry), which contained data on 38 bioclimatic, 8 soil and 3 topographic variables for 48,129 tree species around the world, based on occurrence records for 44 million individual specimens. From this, Kevin was able to extract data that would enable him to model the upper and lower bounds of species-environment relationships and therefore estimate the influence of moisture and temperature on the distribution of species. Using this, along with additional information on hybrids, he calculated the environmental ranges for all the tree species and hybrids growing at Kew – namely the span of average annual temperature, rainfall and PET that each was found growing in – and the lower and upper limits of those variables that those tree taxa could tolerate.

What he needed now was data on the current climate being experienced by trees at Kew, as well as forecasts for future conditions under climate change. He obtained the former from existing databases and the latter from the Intergovernmental Panel on Climate Change (IPCC)'s 6th climate assessment report.

At the United Nations Climate Change Conference held in Paris in 2015, 196 countries had signed a legally binding international treaty known as the Paris Agreement to hold 'the increase in the global average temperature to well below 2°C above pre-industrial levels' and to pursue efforts 'to limit the temperature increase to 1.5°C above pre-industrial levels'. World leaders had subsequently stressed the need to limit global warming to 1.5°C by the end of the century, after the IPCC had concluded that crossing the 1.5°C threshold risked unleashing severe climate change impacts including more frequent and severe droughts, heatwaves and rainfall. However, by early 2023, the global temperature rise in comparison to pre-industrial levels was already running at 1.4°C and was anticipated to breach 1.5°C in the near future; on this basis, Kevin chose the medium-case scenario, known as SSP3.

The forecasts ran to the 2090s, within the likely lifespan of most woody plants – and especially trees. They indicated that, by the end of the century, Kew's climate would be on a par with the current-day climate of Barcelona, in north-east Spain – or indeed Baku in eastern Azerbaijan, Porto in north-west Portugal or Nice in south-east France. The modelled figure for current annual rainfall was around 600mm, with a slight increase forecast by the 2090s. As it gets hotter, trees need more water, so the PET was also predicted to rise. The data indicated that the Gardens today would need 750mm of rain to replenish the moisture evaporated and transpired by its many plants. By the 2050s, this was anticipated to be 800mm and to have risen again to 875mm by the 2090s. These figures took into account the sand and gravel subsoil at the Gardens, which is poor at retaining moisture.

Kevin was able to use observed data from Kew's own weather station located in the heart of the Gardens to validate the model up to 2080. Not only was there a good match with the modelled future results, but the data showed that Kew had already experienced a 3°C rise in average annual temperature between 1981 and 2022, as well as a 300mm fall in yearly rainfall from 900mm in the 1990s to 600mm today. With the modelled PET data indicating that plants across the Gardens currently need 750mm water each year, but the weather station confirming today's annual rainfall to be only 600mm, the data highlighted that Kew was already in water deficit, with plants evaporating and transpiring more moisture than was being naturally replenished. With the PET set to rise but rainfall forecast to stay little more than today, this indicated that Kew's climate would shift from its current temperate-moist climate to a semi-arid environment.

Meanwhile, when Kevin looked at how the rainfall was distributed seasonally at Kew between 1980 and 2022, he found that it had decreased in spring and summer, but increased in autumn and winter. In summer there had been several years when the rainfall had dropped below 100mm across the season. Under the forecast of warmer and drier conditions, this could become a regular feature of summers at Kew. It would present a problem for Kew's trees, as the spring and summer seasons are when they need water to grow. Meanwhile, having more rainfall in autumn and winter could be equally problematic, as soil compaction and less-thirsty plants could either cause flooding locally or cause the water to run off to rivers and the sea. Lately, compaction at Kew has increased at this time of year due to the Garden's expanding programme of late-year events, such as its popular extravaganza, Christmas at Kew. None of this boded well for trees at Kew.

At this point, Kevin began to put his model to the test. Based on the data he had added, it was able to indicate the suitability of any tree species or hybrid to grow at Kew under the environmental conditions indicated for a specified timeframe. Specifically, it was able to state if the species was: 'outside of range' (indicating that the habitat or conditions were unsuitable for the species); only occurred in this zone (in other words, it had not been found growing in conditions outside of this zone, known as 'endemic'); was in the 'upper limits of its range' (at the maximum extent of the species distribution due to the hotter, drier conditions); had reached the 'lower limits of its range' (meaning it could barely survive in this colder, wetter zone and might not be as abundant or successful as it would be in more favourable conditions); or was 'in a wider range', meaning that the zone was contained within the wider 90 per cent distribution range of the taxa – and therefore the species or hybrid was not of concern.

Inputting Kew's lime species to the model yielded some worrying results. Five species, including the small-leaved lime – one of Kew's most numerous species – were indicated to be at the upper limits of their ranges. The results suggested that, under the forecast hotter and drier conditions, these species would not fare well. However, there was a better future signified for trees such as the American basswood (*T. americana*), the Kyushu lime (*T. kiusiana*), the noble lime (*T. nobilis*) and *T. oliveri* – indicated to be at the lower limits of their range at Kew – and for the Chinese lime (*T. chinensis*) and the Crimean lime (*T. dasystyla*), deemed by the model to be within their wider range in the Gardens. Interestingly, the Crimean lime was a companion in the wild to Kevin's favourite tree, the thriving chestnut-leaved oak from the Caucasus. Four of the species, including the silver lime and large-leaved lime (*T. platyphyllos*), came out as 'endemic'. In these cases, the results reflected the limited observation data for them within the model, rather than that the species were constrained to places with a climate akin to that of today at Kew. The drought-tolerant silver lime, for example, is native to warmer and drier south-eastern Europe and north-western Asia.

Although Kevin had originally developed the model for his master's degree, the results clearly had implications for the success of all the trees at Kew. He therefore began to apply it to other species in the Gardens. For 2023, 81 per cent of Kew's woody plants were indicated to be within their natural range for mean annual temperature, with 13 per cent at the edge of their known range and 6 per cent indicated to be outside of their known range. But for the forecast mean annual temperature in 2090 under SSP3, 54 per cent were predicted to be at the edge of or outside of their known range. This is the statistic that had appeared in Kew's Landscape Succession Plan and piqued the interest of the world's media. Among these potential victims of future climate change were the European beech – the beleaguered specimen of which the Tree Gang had had to raze in spring – as well as the English oak. The European beech and English oak are two of the most common trees in UK woodlands today. Interestingly, the critically endangered Wollemi pine (*Wollemia nobilis*), which dates back to the time of the dinosaurs and had been believed extinct until a small population was found in Australia's Blue Mountains in 1994, was predicted to grow better at Kew in future than in its native habitat.

    Kevin and his colleagues used the modelling results to divide species currently growing in the Gardens into 'vulnerable', 'resistant' and 'future resistant'. Vulnerable species were those currently growing in the outdoor living collections that would no longer be within their known environmental range by 2090 under the worst-case scenario (SSP5-8.5). Including the silver birch (*Betula pendula* subspecies *pendula*), common lime (*Tilia* x *europaea*), English oak, saucer magnolia (*Magnolia* x *soulangeana*) and common beech, these were deemed to be potentially poor choices for future planting. Resistant species were those that would be within their environmental range by 2090 under the worst-case scenario, and were therefore considered more robust choices for future planting. These included the holm oak (*Quercus ilex*), Crimean lime (*Tilia dasystyla*), hornbeam (*Carpinus betulus*), golden rain tree (*Koelreuteria paniculata*), oriental plane (*Platanus orientalis*) and hop hornbeam (*Ostrya carpinifolia*). Future resilient species were deemed to be those that had either never been in the temperate living collections or that, if they had and had failed, were worth considering again for potentially replacing vulnerable species. Examples of these included Farges fir (*Abies fargesii*), Iberian alder (*Alnus lusitanica*), cherry hackberry (*Celtis cerasifera*), Montezuma's pine (*Pinus montezumae*) and the spoon oak (*Quercus urbani*).

Much of the seed collecting carried out during Kevin's first decade at the Gardens had been from humid, temperate locations that were well matched with Kew's conditions at the time. These included locations in Japan, China, Vietnam and Taiwan. However, the shift to a hotter, drier climate, coupled with the Gardens' free-draining, poor-quality soil meant that Kew's conditions were no longer matched to those collecting locations. This, Kevin reasoned, helped to explain the forecast loss of so many trees from the Gardens under the much hotter and drier climate scenario. The shift in weather was already being reflected in the visible health of some trees at Kew: redwoods, which thrive in the wild in north California's cool, moist and humid conditions, for example, had been faring badly of late. Meanwhile, trees grown from seeds collected from semi-arid locations – including the Champion and several other chestnut-leaved oaks, holm oaks (*Quercus ilex*) native to the eastern Mediterranean lining the Syon Vista, and trees such as the Italian cypress (*Cupressus sempervirens*) and olive in the Mediterranean Garden – appeared to be thriving. 'We couldn't have got [our past collecting] more wrong,' says Kevin. 'If you talk to the guys who were on those collection trips in China, they'll tell you that when they were there in November it was so humid, they couldn't dry their clothes. So, they were collecting in strong humidity; they weren't thinking about water then, they were worried about cold hardiness.'

Functional traits such as tree height, shape, leaf area, leaf hairiness, flower colour and wood density can sometimes vary across species' geographical ranges. This is particularly the case for species with large ranges that span cold, wet conditions at one end and hot, dry ones at the other. In these, different climate adaptation traits can be present within genotypes of specimens of the same species but from different locations. The natural range of the English oak, for example, extends from the cool temperate forests of northern Europe and western Asia to the warmer, drier Mediterranean habitats of southern Europe and the Caucasus. Surely, if Kew sourced English oaks from the Caucasus, the genotypes of these specimens would endow them with the ability to tolerate the hotter, drier weather encountered there today – and potentially in the future at Kew. If so, they might still be robust planting choices for the future. But how would it be possible to know the best locations to source trees from with the optimal genotypes for Kew's future climate?

Armed with his new-found modelling skills, Kevin went back to his computer, to find locations in which English oaks grow today under weather conditions matching Kew's forecast future climate. Some nifty tech-wrangling made it possible to identify suitable locations within one square kilometre. This meant that he had found a way to pinpoint locations from which Kew could collect specimens of the English oak that would be growing today in a climate akin to Kew's climate in 2090 under the IPCC SSP3 medium-case scenario. Kevin also conducted the same process for other species.

The work highlighted the most suitable locations for Kew to collect from as being southern and western parts of North America, south and west South America, North Africa and southern Spain, the southern tip of Africa, some parts of southern Australia, and a great swathe of Asia, spanning parts of Turkey, Iran, Georgia and Azerbaijan in the west, then extending farther east across Turkmenistan, Uzbekistan, Tajikistan and Kyrgyzstan and onwards into north-western China. Tellingly, the parts of China targeted in the recent past for seed collection by Kew, primarily Sichuan, lying farther east and south, were not indicated as suitable. Taking Kew's poor soils into consideration, steppe environments (a temperate region of grasslands and open woodlands) such as those of the modern-day Caucasus, and the Hyrcanian Forests that wrap round the shores of the Caspian Sea in Iran and Azerbaijan, seemed particularly suitable. And, as it happens, Kew's prize chestnut-leaved oak is native to this latter ecosystem.

With this new-found collecting intelligence, Kevin and Tom Freeth, the Head of Plant Records at Kew, made an exploratory trip to the Romanian steppe in autumn 2023. They hoped to confirm the modelling as an effective way to locate appropriate seed-collection locations. Also, with oaks under particular pressure in southern England, and with Kew keen to ensure the future of its famous and diverse oak collection in light of climate change, their mission was to gather acorns. During the visit they collected those of the downy oak and Hungarian oak so they could conduct a trial of how these species' steppe-derived genotypes might help them be more resilient to drought. They also collected seeds from silver lime, service tree, field maple, hornbeam and small-leaved lime for testing in the Gardens, and to contribute to Kevin's *Tilia* research.

By midsummer 2024, several saplings originating from Romania, including those of *Fagus* x *taurica*, a naturally occurring hybrid of the beeches *F. sylvatica* and *F. orientalis*, are growing well in the Arboretum nursery under the watchful eye of Arboretum Nursery Supervisor Sal Demain. 'The *Fagus* x *taurica* is a really significant tree, when you think that all our common [European] beeches here are really suffering,' says Kevin. '[*Fagus* x *taurica*] grows in Romania in an environment of 500mm of precipitation and 40°C of heat [so has potential to replace European beeches at Kew in the future].'

Trees respond in different ways to stress caused by having too little water. Some are 'stress avoiders', which means they take action to try to stop drought affecting them. Many birches, for example, avoid being affected by drought by closing down their stomata. These are the pores used in photosynthesis, the process by which plants use the energy from sunlight to produce glucose food from carbon dioxide and water. In a persistent drought, a tree will eventually have to open its stomata to photosynthesize – and will then lose water due to transpiration being driven by high vapour pressure deficit (the difference between the vapour pressure of the air when saturated and the actual vapour pressure of the air). This is when the plant can become vulnerable to xylem cavitation; when air pulled into the tree's xylem cuts off the organism's water supply, causing it to die. Other plants are 'stress tolerators'. These are better placed to survive drought, as they are able to adapt to the dry circumstances rather than trying to avoid them. An example is the silver lime *Tilia tomentosa*, the specific epithet of which means 'covered with soft, woolly hairs'. Under particularly arid conditions, the tree inverts its leaves, revealing silvery hairs that reflect the heat better. This action helps the lime to retain moisture and keep its leaves cool so the tree can carry on respiring in the heat.

As summer 2024 advances, Kevin begins to test the leaf turgor loss points of the lime trees at Kew to assess their level of drought tolerance. Pleasingly, he finds that the traits recorded for the different species generally match closely with the model outputs. With the work progressing well, he also starts to investigate the drought tolerance of other species, conducting his experiments in Kew's Jodrell Laboratory, a timber-clad, two-storey building located on the eastern boundary of the Gardens.

On one warm morning, he decides to conduct leaf turgor loss tests on oak leaves because, in his words 'no one has ever tested oak leaves for drought tolerance before'. In the laboratory, a fresh sprig of glossy elongated leaves of a Mexican oak species has been held in place with a sponge in a small, water-filled jar and left in a cool box overnight to rehydrate. Kevin uses a metal punch to cut 5mm leaf discs from the rehydrated leaves, which he wraps in tin foil, and then places in liquid nitrogen for around half an hour to break down the cells. Each individual disc is then transferred to a small white box called a Vapour Pressure Osmometer, which tests the amount of pressure needed to break down the leaf's cell walls. Readings are sent to Kevin's nearby laptop, where they are presented on a bar graph. The graph shows, for example, that Kevin's tested specimen of Chinquapin oak (*Q. prinoides*) has a low turgor loss point (and would therefore be more likely to be able to tolerate drought) and his specimen of English oak has a high turgor loss point and is therefore likely to be less drought tolerant. This prediction for English oak at Kew also matches Kevin's model prediction of the species being 'vulnerable' under Kew's future climate. Soon, though, Kevin's master's is put on hold; he now has so much potential research material his supervisors believe he should consider undertaking a PhD instead.

The reality is that Kevin's work at Kew potentially has applications far beyond the Gardens' walls – for helping urban planners to choose trees to plant with the potential to ameliorate the combined effects of climate change and the 'urban heat island effect'. Increasingly, Kevin is being asked to present his work to urban planners; he recently contributed expertise to the Mayor of London's London Urban Resilience Project, for example, and has also spoken at the House of Lords. When he gives talks, Kevin often shows a high-resolution satellite image from summer 2020, showing the temperature within a seven-square-kilometre area around Kew Gardens. It illustrates, perfectly, the warming effect of cities and the cooling impact of trees. With each square pixel representing 100m^2, and the temperature in each square presented in comparison to average rural temperatures (graded from bright red [hotter] to dark green [cooler]), the image is largely a pixelated mass of red and orange. It points to summer temperatures on the streets of

Richmond, Hounslow and Kew Village being some 3°C higher than those experienced in the countryside. In comparison, the snaking form of the River Thames, where the water pulls down the temperature of the surrounding air, and Richmond Park, which is both higher than the surrounding area and partly wooded, show up as dark green. Kew Gardens ranges from yellow to green, with the centre of the Arboretum registering a temperature of only 0.8°C above rural areas.

The lawn on which Kew's weather station is located clearly stands out from the surrounding green as a bright yellow square, its temperature being higher than that of the rural average by 1.8°C. With no tree canopy nearby to directly intercept the sun's rays, it is the hottest part of the Gardens and is frequently quoted in the UK media as recording the hottest temperature within the country. Kevin jokes that, on one occasion, he and some members of the London Tree Officers Association were having a post-work drink when Kew's Press Department called to ask if Kevin could talk live to the BBC about the hot weather. 'I said "I've just got to the pub", recalls Kevin, 'but they said "It's a great opportunity, would you be up for coming back in?". I just got there in time; they miked me up and said "you've got three minutes". I got my head together a bit then it was "three, two, one and you're live" – and I gave the live interview. Meanwhile, the people I had been meeting with were watching BBC News and up I popped. When I finished the interview, I went back to the pub and finally got my pint.'

Anomalously hot weather is set to affect increasing numbers of people in London and elsewhere as cities expand in the years to come. Globally, the urban population now exceeds the rural one and is anticipated to reach six billion by the 2050s. On particularly hot days, the urban heat island effect could make city life very uncomfortable for those populations. As London had experienced temperatures of over 30°C in early August, several parts of Europe – including Greece, Italy, the Canary Islands, Spain, Turkey and Cyprus – had sweltered in temperatures exceeding 40°C. Tree-covered parts of Europe's cities have been found to cool the land surface temperature by as much as 12°C compared to spaces devoid of trees; green infrastructure is therefore critical to urban planning. However, for trees to be effective natural air conditioners, they must be of the right kind and planted and cared for in the right way.

In his research, Kevin has found an ally in Dr Henrik Sjöman, senior researcher at the Swedish University of Agricultural Sciences and Scientific Curator at Gothenburg Botanical

Garden. Together with garden designer and *BBC Gardeners' World* presenter Arit Anderson, and with a foreword by Kevin, Henrik wrote *The Essential Tree Selection Guide*, outlining how urban planners can best choose trees that will help to keep towns and cities cool in the future. In it, he underlines the importance of understanding the natural environment that tree species have evolved in and then planting trees in city environments that match those conditions. Particular traits of a given tree species can add to its value in terms of its 'ecosystem services', especially in urban areas like that at Kew. When planted and carefully maintained as a part of a diverse tree scheme, a tree that can withstand hot dry conditions in summer, as well as air pollution, and still shade the ground and cool the air around it by continuing to transpire, has much greater value to the urban environment than one which cannot.

Henrik is joining forces with Kevin on fieldwork to gather seeds and laboratory work to test functional traits. Kevin's finding that the common lime is not very drought tolerant is of particular interest, as a study by Henrik and his colleagues showed this hybrid to be the most commonly planted tree in ten Nordic cities, accounting for 16 per cent of the urban trees. Although it is still early days for using plant functional traits in this way, the pair hope that, in time, it might be possible to use evidence from such scientific testing to develop a labelling system for plants. The idea would be to provide a ranking for drought tolerance in much the same way that wine labels currently identify wine from dry to sweet and provide information on grape varieties and provenance. In combination with climate modelling, it would offer a way for urban planners and landscape architects to match tree genotypes to predicted future climatic conditions and the ecosystem-service needs of their particular cityscape. 'If you go for [trees that are] "stress avoiders" that lockdown when a drought arises, they can actually increase the temperatures in city centres,' warns Kevin. 'That's why this work we're doing at Kew is so important. It's not just about understanding how we're going to manage the landscape here over the next 100 years but it's also vitally important for urban environments. That's what all my research is based on – looking at how we can use botanic gardens to influence urban planting.'

While Kevin is busy researching trees for the future Kew Gardens and beyond, the rest of the Tree Gang have the job of dealing with the day-to-day tasks around the Gardens. With the hot summer weather now attracting increasing numbers of visitors, they have to carefully decide where to work and what to do. They choose an overcast morning when the Gardens are not too busy to remove an irregularly shaped stump of a silver maple (*Acer saccharinum*) – a common tree from the eastern and central USA. The tree had stood in front of the Temperate House since 1897 but over time had become unsafe due to decay, and so the Gang had cut it down. A few months later, the stump's pale wood is mottled with grey and rust-coloured patches. Tom concludes that the tree probably succumbed to honey fungus, a complex of *Armillaria* species that can affect trees and shrubs. Living within plant root systems, it is often heralded by the appearance of honey-coloured toadstools at the base of woody plants in autumn and can also be identified from white growths under the bark and dark bootlace-like threads in the soil. A honey fungus has the distinction of being the largest single living organism on Earth: located in the Malheur National Forest in eastern Oregon, USA, the 'Humungous Fungus' covers 9.6 square kilometres (3.7 square miles) and may be 8,000 years old.

Because honey fungus can stay in the soil even after its main host has been removed, Tom decides to remove as much of the stump as possible and then cover over the space with soil. The ground will need to be left for some time before replanting – if at all. The Gang have a brand-new, bright-red stump cutter, and removing the maple is an opportunity to familiarize themselves with the novel tool. After fencing off the site, Tom drives the tractor-pulled stump-grinder into place. Then he fires up the cutter, operating it from a joystick at the rear of the tractor's cab. Its vertical cutting wheel begins to rotate, speeding up until practically invisible. When Tom brings it down on the stump, and moves it slowly from side to side, it slices through the wood with ease, sending out a fine cloud of brown dust from under a chain-mail guard. Despite the noise and violence of the wheel, it is a delicate operation to place the cutter exactly where needed and to the right depth.

After five or so minutes, when half the stump has been ground down, it's Jamie's turn to take the controls. This is a valuable opportunity for the members of the Gang at work today to try out this new piece of equipment and to practise the health and safety required for such a task in a public space. It also provides a welcome break for them from the very physical job of climbing trees. 'For us, as humans, the heat in the summer affects us quite a bit sometimes, and we have to start at 6am just to beat the heat especially with all the PPE that we wear, so it can get quite horrendous,' explains Jamie. This doesn't rule out tree climbing 'but some of the subtle improvement works that we do are very dependent on the seasonal weather,' he explains. Today, with the new stump cutter having excelled at turning timber to dust, the only physical work left for the Gang to do is carefully rake over the ground.

A few weeks later, Tom, Rich, Will and Jamie attend a demonstration of a battery-powered wood chipper. In its 2021 Sustainability Strategy, Kew had committed to going beyond net zero to become climate positive by 2030, and all departments are finding ways to contribute to achieving this. In using their electric chainsaws and buggy rather than diesel kit the Gang are already helping to cut Kew's carbon emissions, but there is more to be done. After their morning coffee break, the group gather in the Stable Yard, where a gleaming red chipper awaits their examination. It's smaller than the current diesel-driven machine the Gang use but, they are assured by the manufacturer's representative who has come to demonstrate its capabilities, it can work for five hours on a full battery and can be recharged in seven hours. 'I think it's about time we put something through it,' he says, after a few minutes.

He presses a large yellow button and the machine quietly starts up. Close by, a tractor rumbles past to drop off a trailer-load of prunings, while a JCB digger nudges steaming piles of compost into high mounds. Will offers up a section of branch to the wood chipper. Although it is several centimetres thick, the machine readily draws the branch inside through a black metal roller beyond which spinning teeth can be seen through a clear plastic shield. There's a pause, and then the machine spits out chunky sawdust through the outlet pipe in noisy pulses. It's capable of taking branches up to 175mm thick, the demonstrator explains. After taking it in turns to feed the machine, Tom and the team head back to the workshop. They're impressed by the chipper and feel that battery-powered tech is definitely improving. Nonetheless, this model is not quite powerful enough to cope with the size of timber that Kew regularly needs to chip. The general consensus is that 'it's less of a gatling gun, and more of a woodpecker on speed'.

As new pieces of equipment regularly become available, and new regulations and ideas frequently emerge, training, for the Tree Gang, is a constant necessity in order to keep up to date. Summer is often the best time for this, as not only can working at height wearing protective gear in the heat be physically exhausting, but pruning at this time of year can cause additional stress to trees already under pressure in warm, dry conditions – so both are best avoided. Training has long been a key component of work for the gardeners and arborists at Kew. Indeed, just as a place on the Kew Apprenticeship in Arboriculture is sought-after today, so, for 19th-century gardeners and arborists, a certificate for Kew's two-year course of study and a recommendation from the Gardens held great sway in the job market both here and overseas.

The older trees in the Arboretum are a living library of how these historic gardeners used what were then considered to be the best techniques. Some trees, such as the Japanese pagoda tree near the Hive, are particularly noticeable for having been subject to a plethora of now out-of-date practices. This once tall tree has only one side branch remaining, which rests recumbent on several bespoke steel props. The base of its trunk is supported by a neat wall of bricks, it has had Arbrex (a more modern version of the tar once used) painted on previous pruning wounds, and on the side away from public view it has even had expanding foam forced into its trunk. Most of this treatment is not as old as might be assumed, since photos from around 1900 show the tree simply being held up by wooden props. Despite its life of adversity, this remarkable Old Lion continues to grow and flower each year.

One of Tom's favourite trees, a characterful veteran hornbeam not far from the Stable Yard, has also had an eventful life at the hands of previous arborists. 'It's got things like cavities, it's got this massive base, and it's got these long fissures in it, but it's also got drainpipes inside it,' he enthuses. 'It's got static steel cable [bracing] across it, and all these weird features that were considered the best practice in the day. This is the great thing about working here, because you can see [what they tried and] where they went wrong. You are part of that history, and you can see the evolution over the last hundred-plus years when people really started managing trees. [In the past, if they encountered] a fork in a tree and water was pooling in that fork, they thought "you need to get that water out because the water will decay the wood", so they drilled a hole and put a drainpipe through it, but that is the complete opposite of what should happen. The water is keeping the oxygen out, preventing decay.'

Like Tom, Jamie also looks out for the work of previous arborists when he climbs trees at Kew, including pruning cuts that are flush to the main trunk, which is, he says, 'a big no-no these days'. Today the Tree Gang carry out what is called target pruning, popularized by American forester and plant pathologist Dr Alex Shigo in the 1980s, which recommends that the branch collar is left in place when you prune off a branch rather than cutting flush to the stem. Shigo, of the US Department of

Agriculture Forest Service, who is known by some as the father of modern arboriculture, recognized that trees could seal and heal their own wounds if cut this way because the tissues within the branch collar were connected to the main trunk and not the branch being cut, allowing a new wall of tissue to cover the wound. This also meant that the use of paints and tars – once seen as a way of preventing infection getting into pruning cuts – was completely unnecessary and in fact only sealed fungi in, giving them a better environment to grow in.

Shigo's research on decay and wound healing in trees was scientifically proven and this method is used now by all professional gardeners and arborists. Such work has since been built upon, and a range of improved techniques and research introduced, including those proposed by Professor Claus Mattheck, who lectures in biomechanics and researches tree form and failure at the Karlsruhe Research Centre in Germany. Using the latest best practices, the care of trees at Kew has been transformed over the 20th century.

That is not to say that the work of previous arborists is not greatly admired here. The work of the Tree Gang today is built upon what those pioneers discovered, practised and achieved. In fact, former head of the Arboretum William Jackson Bean and his assistant William Dallimore (who worked here in the late 19th and early 20th centuries) are heroes of the Tree Gang. Bean, the son of a tree nurseryman, joined Kew in 1883 as a student gardener, rose to become Arboretum Foreman in 1892, and eventually served as Curator between 1922 and 1929. Bean's most famous book – the multi-volume *Trees and Shrubs Hardy in the British Isles* was a labour of love, grounded in detailed observations and correspondence, personal assessments of plants, references to particular specimens at Kew, and his own reminiscences. It went on to eight editions and is still used today.

Dallimore began his working life in a plant nursery in Lancashire at just 13 years old. He came to Kew as a student gardener in 1891, where he diligently followed the Kew training syllabus for two years, after which he was assigned to the Arboretum as a propagator and later foreman under Bean in 1896. He would go on to become Kew's Keeper of the Museums, during which time he also took on the creation and management of Kew's first sister garden, Bedgebury Pinetum in Kent. During his career, Dallimore developed key techniques in propagation, tree climbing and pruning; built the collections and Kew's international reputation with Bean; and wrote five books and many articles, including *The Handbook of Coniferae* in 1923 and *The Pruning of Trees and Shrubs* in 1926. He also helped start the Kew Guild, connecting Kew staff and students past and present. He sat on government committees, developed a museum of British forestry at Kew, and received both the Veitch Memorial Medal and the Victoria Medal of Honour from the Royal Horticultural Society. No wonder he was known as 'good old Dally'.

Old black-and-white photographs on the wall of the Tree Gang's workshop recall the early days in the collections. In one particularly famous image, a young Dallimore, bedecked with all the tools of his job, stares at the camera, almost challenging the viewer to try to match his achievements. The men who started Kew's tree teams are rightly famous in the history of British arboriculture as they were pioneers in many techniques that are still used today. Curators such as George Nicholson, followed by Bean and Dallimore and then by Arthur Osborn, were key in that regard. Each was important in changing the face of the Arboretum and how it was practically managed. All of these men wrote seminal works about trees and their care, based on their practical experiences at Kew, which, as Kevin's research into the trees of the Caucasus shows, are still being referenced and remain relevant today.

By the late 19th century – when the Arboretum had been initially designed and planted – Kew was a centre of developing knowledge about arboriculture. It is hard to comprehend now, but little was then known and taught about how best to propagate, plant, prune, irrigate and manage a large taxonomic collection of trees. While there was a great tradition of forestry and fruit-tree management in Britain, there was little information about looking after ornamental or 'exotic' trees. John Claudius Loudon's *The Gardener's Magazine* (founded in 1826) and his eight-volume *Arboretum Britannicum* (1838) sought to overcome this for the working gardener, and these publications were often to be found in small libraries available to the gardeners. Kew's library was situated in the building now used as offices next to the Director's House on Kew Green. Here, gardeners could not only read the latest magazines and books but also make use of a warm fire on a winter's evening.

The small team appointed to look after Kew's trees in the latter half of the 19th century consulted books from France and Germany (then leaders in arboriculture) about how to prune. However, they still had to work through trial and error as they built up Kew's tree collections. A solid network of head gardeners and nurserymen throughout the country also shared knowledge and practices both through correspondence and the growing gardening press. New techniques in tree surgery such as those recommended by expert consultant Denis Le Sueur were tried, tested and incorporated into Kew's practices.

Tree climbing remained a primitive affair throughout the 19th century however, with the use of climbing spikes attached to the inner lower legs (even though they were known to damage the tree), waist belts or a cord around the middle, ropes (for pulling up tools), tapered ladders, and occasionally built platforms. Axes and saws remained the tools of choice. Such techniques, as described by Mark Johnston, were, remarkably, not to change significantly until the 1960s, despite Le Sueur trying to introduce safety belts and slings from France and North America in the 1930s. New safety harnesses were promoted by tree surgery firms in the 1960s and 1970s, but it is only in the last 20 years that extraordinary progress has been made in the types of rope, harness, and many other items of safety equipment for arborists – and more recently still that women arborists have been able to buy gender-specific kit.

Just as gardeners in previous centuries were expected to make time for researching the plant collections they worked with and to keep up to date with new practices, so today's Tree Gang are also encouraged to do their own research. Each member of the Gang has chosen a different genus of tree to explore in the Arboretum. While Tom has selected oaks, Jamie has chosen *Abies* – the evergreen conifers commonly known as the firs, which are some of the most important conifers in the northern hemisphere. There are roughly 60 species of *Abies*, four of which are critically endangered. One of these – the Baishan fir (*Abies beshanzuensis*) is the most endangered conifer in the world. 'I chose *Abies* as they were my favourite trees at the time, they're very prehistoric-looking,' says Jamie, 'but also they intrigued me as they are difficult to grow here and there is some interesting conservation work going on around the world.' *Abies* also have very beautiful cones, which stand upright on their branches. Some writers have described these as akin to botanical Fabergé eggs. Some of Jamie's favourite trees in the Gardens include a particular group of three Japanese Nikko firs (*Abies homolepis*) near the Lake, 'which have this kind of bubble wrap bark on their tall straight trunks, which I have never seen on any other members of that species,' he says.

Since their inception, botanic gardens have been places for learning and for the development and sharing of knowledge, but the focus of that knowledge has changed over the past few hundred years. During the European colonial era, such gardens sought to gather scientific and horticultural collections from across the temperate world and to create a taxonomically arranged landscape for the advancement of science and empire. During this period, Kew's Arboretum was a living laboratory, testing out new species to see how they grew in

Britain and using them to further botanical science, forestry, trade and education about trees. Each tree was labelled to be of educational use to both visitors and scientists.

Over the 20th century, as society and culture changed, so did the purposes of the Arboretum. After the death of empire and two world wars, social needs shifted rapidly. From the mid-20th century, conservation of species and habitat restoration became a driving force for Kew, culminating in its current mission to tackle the twin planetary emergencies of biodiversity loss and climate change. Today, trees have never been in more peril, with more than one in three tree species worldwide threatened with extinction. Yet, faced with climate change, understanding trees and the benefits they can bring us has never been more important. It is serendipitous that Kew's Arboretum, with collections from all over the world, provides the perfect living resource for tackling such global crises. Or as Kevin sees it, 'the biggest thing that has come out of my research for the organization is the importance of the Arboretum.' The hope is that the current and future generations of curious and diligent scientists, with the benefit of state-of-the-art laboratories and DNA-level understanding of plants, can use this enduring arboreal laboratory to set the world's environment on a better path, and help humans learn to live in the warmer world they have created.

Part Three
AUTUMN

As September draws to a close, the Arboretum is perceptibly changing. The fan-shaped leaves of the old *Ginkgo biloba* growing near the Hive are turning a buttery yellow. The maples near the Shirley Sherwood Gallery are starting their annual transition to crimson. And the *Liquidambar* trees near Kew Palace are beginning to live up to their name. With sunlight less abundant in the shortening days, the chlorophyll that has been lending leaves their verdant summer hues is breaking down to reveal a new palette of fiery pigments. The onset of autumn means the race is on for trees to reproduce, too. In the first strong winds of the season, sycamores fling out spinning samaras, oaks shake acorns from their protective cups and horse chestnuts bounce conkers from their spiky seed cases.

These visual cues mean only one thing for Kevin. It's the perfect time for a seed-collecting expedition to Georgia in the Caucasus region. Although the country experiences the same four seasons as the UK, the hotter, drier summer there lingers a little longer, making the first few weeks of October the perfect time to gather ripe seeds. And, as Kevin's research has indicated, trees that have grown up in more arid climes, such as Georgia's, might just hold the key to keeping Kew's Arboretum thriving as London warms and desiccates in the coming decades. Armed with a wish list of trees to collect from, which includes limes for his research, as well as oaks, beeches and hornbeams for Kew's living collection, Kevin flies to Tbilisi, together with Tom and Arboretum Nursery Supervisor Sal. They are partnering with Gothenburg Botanical Garden in their mission, so in Tbilisi they meet up with Henrik, as well as with Emil Wallin, who is head of the nursery at Gothenburg Botanical Garden. The five of them will take a three-week road trip across Georgia, gathering seeds from the country's temperate mixed forests as they go.

Georgia lies at the meeting point of Europe and Asia. It is crossed by the Caucasus mountains that run in two parallel chains, 100 kilometres (62 miles) apart, west-north-west to east-south-east between the Black and the Caspian seas. The Greater Caucasus separate northern Georgia and neighbouring Azerbaijan from Russia, while the Lesser Caucasus divide southern Georgia from north-east Turkey and northern Armenia. As their names suggest, the Greater Caucasus are higher, with several peaks exceeding 5,000 metres (16,400 feet) and a permanent icing of snow and glaciers. The Lesser

Caucasus rise to just over 4,000 metres (13,000 feet). Their less lofty elevation means that they have no glaciers, and only seasonal snowfall that melts in the summer. The two ranges host a huge tapestry of habitats that make them a hotspot of plant diversity; they support 6,400 species altogether, more than a quarter of which do not grow anywhere else. Although the Caucasus cross six countries in all, Georgia is of particular interest to the visiting arborists. Not only does it host some 150 tree species (around three times more than the UK) but they grow in habitats that are relatively close together and straightforward to access.

The make-up of the woodlands that cover large parts of the Caucasus ranges is broadly dictated by altitude. Between 400 and 1,000 metres (1,312 and 3,281 feet) above sea level, broadleaf forests flourish. These include warmth-loving Mediterranean species, such as the olive, bay laurel (*Laurus nobilis*) and Mediterranean cypress as well as the Georgian oak (*Quercus petraea* subspecies *polycarpa*), which grows wild between Austria and Iran, and the Egyptian balsam (*Balanites aegyptiaca*), native to much of Africa and parts of the Middle East. From 1,000 to 1,500 metres' elevation (3,281 to 4,922 feet), the suite of species more closely resembles that of the UK's current native flora, including species such as the English oak,

European beech, small-leaved lime and the Scots pine (*Pinus sylvestris*). With Georgia representing the drier, warmer eastern extent of these species' range, it is the flora of this slice of uplands that Kevin hopes might keep UK native species thriving at Kew – and potentially in cities across currently temperate Europe – in future. Meanwhile, above 1,500 metres (4,922 feet), cold-loving conifers such as the Caucasian spruce (*Picea orientalis*) and Nordmann fir (*Abies nordmanniana*) – a favourite Christmas tree choice in the UK – come into their own.

The first port of call for the group is Georgia's main botanical institution, the Niko Ketskhoveli Institute of Botany (IoB) of Ilia State University, located in a futuristic-looking white building on a steep valley side overlooking the National Botanical Garden of Georgia (NBGG). Having visited the Institute many times while researching the suitability of Georgian trees for use in urban landscapes in Sweden, Henrik is already acquainted with its Director, Professor Shalva 'Nukri' Sikharulidze, and Deputy Director, David Kikodze. He has arranged a meeting with them to check whether any permits will be required to collect plant material, and to pick their brains about the best sites from which to collect seeds of species on their wish lists. On collecting expeditions like these, the timing of trees' seed dispersal is everything, so local knowledge is key. Like Kevin, Henrik seeks potentially drought-tolerant ecotypes of European trees (an ecotype being a population adapted to particular conditions, underpinned by the genotypes of its individual members), as well as new species to showcase in Gothenburg Botanical Garden. The meeting is also an opportunity for the members of the Tree Gang in attendance to meet Nukri and David, and to forge a direct link with the IoB. Although Kew's Millennium Seed Bank (MSB) has an established partnership with the Institute, it is Kevin's, Tom's and Sal's first visit to the IoB – and to Georgia.

Everyone is welcomed to a large meeting room adjoining Nukri's office and offered cakes and mineral water. Georgia boasts more than 700 mineral-water springs, and this natural commodity is an important export. These resources also give Tbilisi its name: it means 'warm place', a reference to the thermal baths for which the city is famous. Henrik gives Nukri an ornamental owl as a gift – which he says reminds him of the Director's wisdom – before explaining that the group are on a quest to find seeds that will yield trees suitable for the future climes of both London and Gothenburg. 'Our ultimate aim is to collect seeds of particular species and test their whole range from Ireland to Georgia,' he explains. 'We want to evaluate them for heat tolerance to see what native species fit

England and Sweden the best. We're going to grow some in the gardens and we will torture some in the greenhouse to see what conditions they can tolerate. And, at Gothenburg, we'll use some to show visitors trees from the Caucasus.'

Nukri confirms that it's a good time to collect seeds. Then he, David and Henrik pore over a road map of Georgia. After much debate, the decision is taken; the group will first drive east to explore the drier, lowlands areas of eastern Georgia. From there, they will head west towards Gori, which is less dry and, in places, more humid. Gori is renowned as the birthplace of Joseph Stalin, who led the Soviet Union for three decades from 1924 and of which Georgia formed part between 1921 and 1991. Thereafter, the group will drive towards the Russian border to visit the forested uplands around Oni, before descending towards subtropical Batumi on the Black Sea coast. They are hoping that the hills in this far south-west part of the country might reveal the very rare Pontine oak (*Quercus pontica*). From there they will complete the circle back to Tbilisi. Nukri and David provide a letter written in Georgian for the visitors, which explains who the group are and the aims of their fieldwork in case anyone stops them. Such assistance is invaluable, as an official unable to comprehend why a party of Brits and Swedes are climbing trees in the middle of a Georgian forest could easily put paid to a trip like this.

In a world in which two in five plants are threatened with extinction – including a third of all tree species – strong partnerships between botanic gardens are vital. Kew's relationship with Georgia dates back two decades, when the MSB first signed a Protocol of Collaboration with the IoB and NBGG. Since then, Kew and these Georgian partners have collaborated on several mutually beneficial projects to document and conserve Georgian plants. An example is a three-year project that sought to conserve important wild fruit and nut species – such as the common hazel (*Corylus avellana*), oriental hawthorn (*Crataegus orientalis*) and blackthorn (*Prunus spinosa*) – and to support rural communities who use the plants for foods and medicines to do so sustainably. As part of the collaboration, Kew trained staff at the IoB and NBGG in techniques to conserve seeds and to assess the risk of individual species becoming extinct. In exchange, Kew scientists were introduced to local communities and were able to gather seeds and other plant material to conserve and research in the MSB.

David is currently coordinating the IoB's part of a major MSB initiative – The Weston Global Tree Seed Bank: Unlocked. This is the fourth phase of a project seeking to conserve many of the rarest and most threatened woody species across the world. The first three phases, which took place between 2014 and 2023 and focused on conservation, saw seeds of 3,500 species gathered from 40 countries and territories, including Georgia. The fourth phase, which will run for three years, is expanding the focus to both conserving species and restoring habitats. The Georgian aspect of this phase has three main objectives. The first is to collect and conserve two genetically distinct collections from 14 species that are currently not banked at the MSB. The second is to gather seeds from up to four populations of species already in the MSB to expand the overall genetic diversity and make 'restoration-ready collections' – including of the much-loved Nordmann fir. And the third is to develop seed-storage protocols for three ivy (*Hedera*) species that have proven difficult to conserve using traditional seed-banking methods of drying seeds and storing them at low temperatures. Kew, the IoB and the NBGG are working closely together to fulfil the work.

'Since 2005, Kew has been our number one partner,' declares David. 'From our side, it helps us to be working with this world-famous institution. It's great to have access to modern technology and guidelines that ease our lives – because good standards and methodologies at an international level are something we lack from Soviet times. Also, financial support and technology transfer allow us to pay our staff and keep them doing science. And Kew gets really unique plant material from us because the Caucasus region is one of the biodiversity hotspots of the world. It's a mutual benefit that we know our genetic resources are preserved at Kew. Road construction, pipeline building and development mean that there is lots of pressure on the plant life here, and, as botanists, it's really key for us to make sure we have enough material preserved in case we need to reintroduce extinct species or to reinforce populations that are under the threat of extinction. Also, Kew botanists have the chance to travel to Georgia and to familiarize themselves with the flora and the landscapes of the country, and I like to believe that Georgia is also an important partner for Kew.'

As today's IoB meeting draws to a close, with new connections successfully forged, Nukri and David lead the visitors through patio doors to a terrace that looks across the city. Following the skyline from north-west to north-east offers up a lesson in Tbilisi's history. Close by to the north-west is Sololaki Ridge, on top of which stands *Kartlis Deda*, 'Mother of Georgians'. This 20-metre-high aluminium figure holds a bowl of wine in her left hand to welcome visitors and a sword in her right to fend off enemies; down the centuries, the city has been captured and sacked by many groups, including the Persians, Byzantines, Arabs and Mongols. The statue was erected in 1958 when Tbilisi celebrated the 1,500th anniversary of its founding in the 5th century by King Vakhtang I of Kartli. The king allegedly built a fortress, where today, in the near foreground to the northeast, the much later 16th- and 17th-century walls of Narikala Fortress now dominate the view. Above them, the Orthodox Church of St Nicholas stands tall. Originally constructed in the 13th century by Demetrius II, this current incarnation of the church is less than 30 years old. Desecrated in 1818 and turned into a munitions dump by the brutal and bloodthirsty Russian Imperial General Yermolov, the original building was destroyed when the dump exploded. It was only rebuilt, to its predecessor's design and reusing the materials from the rubble, after archaeologists uncovered its remains in 1966.

The spires of cypress trees dotting the city and wooded hills on its distant edge are a reminder that the arborists have work to do, so, at midday, they thank their hosts and set off on foot back to their hotel. The journey takes them down the steep cobbled hill of Botanikuri Street, between the colourful, balconied houses of Tbilisi's old town, and then uphill past grand old terraced buildings to the Communal Hotel Sololaki. Here, everyone piles into a hire car and they set off for Tbilisi National Park, around an hour's drive to the north. It's a chance for Kevin, Tom and Sal to see the wild Georgian flora for the first time, assess how this season's seed yield is looking and try out the new, lightweight climbing kit they have bought especially for the trip. Henrik, who has volunteered to be the expedition's driver, joins the weaving traffic around Freedom Square – where a golden statue of St George slaying a dragon has replaced one of Lenin that was razed when the Soviet Union broke up in 1991 – then heads out of town on Shota Rustaveli Avenue, named after a famous medieval Georgian poet.

    The journey along this main thoroughfare provides a sharp contrast to the old town of earlier, the car passing the arched façade of the Georgian Parliament on the left, museums and the neo-Moorish building of the Opera and Ballet Theatre of Tbilisi on the right, and plentiful Western shops such as Zara and MAC Cosmetics. During the drive, expedition tasks are allocated among the group. Everyone will help to collect, count and clean seeds, as required. Tom and Kevin will share the tree climbing between them, Henrik and Emil will gather other material for preserving to make herbarium vouchers for Gothenburg, and Sal will take field notes and use the GPS device to record the exact location of each collection. In addition, Kevin will also collect data for his own research. Soon, Henrik turns off the busy highway onto a narrow road that winds uphill through woodland. 'This is steppe forest,' he explains. 'It has the same trees as western Europe but these are more drought tolerant. There are a lot of oaks and elms and the oriental hornbeam (*Carpinus orientalis*). It's the most easterly part of the Colchic flora [the name referencing the ancient Colchis region of Western Georgia]. In spring you'll see *Galanthus* [snowdrops] and in the evergreen mid-layer you can see *Ilex* [holly].'

Everyone expectantly scans the woodland scenes sliding slowly past the windows. Soon, the first specimens of oriental beech (*Fagus orientalis*) and the Cappadocian maple (*Acer cappadocicum*) come into view, growing from a steep bank of gravel that exposes both the tree roots and pebbles. The small size of the trees suggests that the conditions here are sufficiently dry for them to need to play safe when it comes to hydraulics; having less far to distribute water around their structures will help them avoid the potential for xylem cavitation by overdrawing moisture from the dry soil.

As the environment gets damper with altitude, however, the arborists are quick to spot responding changes in the vegetation. The oriental hornbeam prevalent lower down is usurped by the European hornbeam (*Carpinus betulus*). Higher still, the trees get bigger; clearly they now have more confidence in the available moisture resources. Near the top, the bird cherry (*Prunus avium*) and the broadleaf spindle tree (*Euonymus latifolius*) come into sight, both of which like to stretch out their roots in moist but well-drained soils. Henrik parks up beside a shrine at the foot of a giant scaffolding cross before leading the group uphill to where Zedazeni Monastery sits on the hill's apex.

At the top, the controlling influences of temperature and moisture on woody species become even more apparent. At the apex of this north-facing slope are oriental beech, European hornbeam, bird cherry and common ash; all trees that favour cooler, more moist conditions. But just six or eight metres away, on the southern slope of the hill, it's a different story. Looking in this direction over the stone monastery boundary wall, towards where the afternoon sun is glinting off the distant Kura River, the five see mixed woodlands of oriental hornbeam, sessile oak, cornelian cherry (*Cornus mas*), manna ash (*Fraxinus ornus*), cherry plum (*Prunus cerasifera*), field maple (*Acer campestre*) and wild service tree (*Sorbus torminalis*); all species with an element of in-built drought tolerance.

The way the vegetation changes over such a small distance demonstrates how a three-pronged approach could be the best way to source trees for Europe's future botanical gardens and urban areas. Firstly, modelling can be used to locate an area likely to have trees of suitable ecotypes. Secondly, trained botanists employing local knowledge are vital for identifying appropriate specimens from which to gather seeds. And thirdly, laboratory tests of traits such as turgor loss point can provide the scientific evidence to quantify the level of drought tolerance imprinted in an individual specimen's genes. 'These three things together can make a very strong case to take to nurseries and landscape architects, and to create confidence for planners,' says Henrik. 'We need to produce some clear evidence, as it's a big thing to go from the known to the unknown when it comes to using less traditional trees in urban planning. The climate here, particularly on the south side, is the kind of environment that we're going to see in London and Berlin and Copenhagen in a hundred years,' he continues. 'Some of these species we have in Europe, but here [in Georgia] they already have developed a tolerance to drought compared to trees in the UK. The new plant hunting is therefore aimed at finding different genetic material within species; and the science to support that is available now.'

Keen to take a closer look at the flora, the group return a short way down the north-facing side of the hill, and head into the woodland on foot beside a monument carved with three stylized goats. They climb steeply up a stony path, shaded by the autumnal woodland canopy, before stopping at a large oriental beech. This species is of interest to Kevin as it is thought to lend drought tolerance to *Fagus* x *taurica*, the natural hybrid of *F. sylvatica* and *F. orientalis* that he has already collected seeds from in Romania. Here in the National Park, Tom will climb the tree and check if the seeds are mature. Kevin throws a thin rope over a high branch, waits for Tom to attach his turquoise, orange and yellow climbing line to the far end of it, and then reels it in. Once the rope is doubled over the branch, Tom ties a 'bowline on a bight' knot at one end to secure a base anchor. Then he begins to climb on the other end, using his friction device and foot ascender. The rope is only 37 metres long and the tree is considerably higher, so Tom has to reposition the anchor once he reaches the lower branches. Upwards he climbs, until the canopy closes below him, and he disappears from view. 'I can see seeds and the masts [fruits] are open,' he announces from on high. 'They're just falling out at the slightest touch.'

The tree is growing in a gully, a favoured environment of beech due to its need for moisture. Adjacent trees have had to compete to get above the steep gully sides up into the sunlight, causing them to grow tall and creating a high canopy. Although it's a beautiful afternoon, only dappled sunlight reaches down to the forest floor, keeping the understorey cool. With dark green ivy creeping along the ground and up trunks it feels much like the woodlands of the UK's South Downs, but there are subtle differences, such as clumps of variegated cyclamen leaves punching through the accumulated leaf litter. High above, the wind pushes branches around with a quiet, static-like hiss. In order to examine some of the seeds that are steadily falling from the tree, a tarpaulin is spread out. Sal picks up a brown beech seed, which is three-sided, with a rounded bottom, pointed top, and paler colouring at the seams. It appears to have had small holes drilled in it by a weevil. 'When we are collecting seeds to bring back to the Arboretum Nursery, we'll do a "sink test" in the evening [by putting the seeds in water] – and disregard those that float [and which are not likely to be viable],' says Sal. 'We need to be careful we don't introduce any bugs to Kew.'

This is 53-year-old Sal's first collecting trip, although she's been at Kew for nine years. After leaving her home city of Salford, Greater Manchester, to complete a foundation course in Arts and Crafts at Exeter College, Devon, in her early 20s, she went on to become a bar manager but gained an RHS Level 2 qualification in horticulture at evening classes. This led to her setting up her own gardening business in Portugal, tending to everything from small container gardens to expansive orange groves, and propagating plants to sell on to her clients. One day, when she was walking along the cliffs between Praia de Amoreira and Praia da Carreagem in Aljezur, she noticed the sculpted nature of the flora and realized that plants she usually saw growing large in gardens were only a foot high in their wild habitat due to being naturally 'wind-pruned'.

It was an epiphanous moment. Thereafter Sal became more interested in how plants grow in nature, and she started to embrace the naturally dry conditions of the Algarve by focusing more on gravel gardens. She also studied for the RHS Level 3 qualification, returning to the UK to take exams every six months. Eventually she came back to the UK for good, and was offered a job at Hollesley Bay Prison, Suffolk, teaching horticulture to inmates. However, an unexpected but fortuitous turn of fate led to her studying for the Kew Diploma in Horticulture instead. 'I accidentally came to Kew,' she recalls. 'It took six months for the prison to vet me because I'd been out of the country, during which time I saw the advert for the Kew Diploma. I thought it would be nice to have a day out at the Gardens, so I came and did the interview and they offered me a place. I was living in Suffolk at the time and I thought, "Oh I don't really want to go and live in London". I spent the first six months after I'd been accepted moaning that I didn't want to live in London and then as soon as I walked through the door I thought, "I never want to leave this place".'

The diploma involved Sal studying for three years, with three months of each year spent attending lectures at the School of Horticulture and the rest of the time gaining experience in different departments, including the Arboretum, Gardens, Display Glasshouses and Tropical Nursery. On graduating in 2019, she spent three years working in the Arboretum and Tropical Nurseries as a Botanical Horticulturist before being promoted to her current supervisory role in August 2022. Just before she came to Georgia, Kew's staff structure was reorganized, bringing Sal under Kevin's management – and making her officially a member of the Tree Gang. 'Kevin is now my line manager which aligns more with the planned future of the outside space at Kew,' she explains. 'The Arboretum

Nursery historically used to be mostly concerned with trees and woody collections. Over the years we've started to do more than that but I think we need to refocus on the tree collections and align with the Landscape Succession Plan. It will change the role for the better because there will be more of a focus on conservation, so it's an exciting time to be leading a team in the Nursery. And we've got more staff as well so we can do more propagation. So hopefully it will change my role. We will be doing more interesting propagation; more grafting and sowing naturally sourced material.'

Sal's first experience of gathering such material for Kew is to begin the following day – but not until the group have tucked into a mighty Georgian breakfast to rival the Bartlett team's spread following the oak processionary moth spraying in May. The breakfast, which the hotel's Head Host Giorgi Poplavski boasts is the best in Tbilisi, includes: a variety of fresh breads; cold meats; hard-boiled eggs; tomato, feta and cucumber salads; olives; cheeses, including the slightly sour and salty *sulguni* (the best cheese in the world, according to Giorgi); sweet watermelon-skin jam; and *churchkhela*, a Georgian speciality made by dipping strings of walnuts in boiling grape juice thickened with flour and leaving them to dry outside in the shade. The meal sets the arborists up well for their journey, which begins with a short stop near Akhmeta to see the rare Caucasian elm (*Zelkova carpinifolia*) in Babaneuri Strict Nature Reserve. It is not, in fact, an elm but belongs to the same family as elms, the Ulmaceae. Some 6,000 to 5,500 years ago, *Zelkova* forests were widespread in the Caucasus but deforestation and clearance for farming mean that only patchy populations remain in the country.

Today, the Caucasian elm is listed by the International Union for the Conservation of Nature (IUCN) as globally 'vulnerable', with populations decreasing. The tree is medium- to large-sized, with small, oval leaves that are bright copper at this time of year. Although there are quite a few already growing back at Kew, most of them are the clone known as *Z. carpinifolia* 'James Gordon' (as with *Ginkgo biloba* and *Styphnolobium japonicum*, Gordon was the first person in Britain to grow *Z. carpinifolia* in his London nursery, although it is not clear how he came by his source material). The clones derived from Gordon's early endeavours, many of which ended up growing in botanic gardens, are 'fastigiate' – meaning they are 'vase-shaped' with branches growing more or less parallel to the main trunk – and for years botanists thought that this was the natural appearance of *Z. carpinifolia*. In fact, specimens growing in the wild generally have fewer upright branches and more rounded crowns, and Kevin is keen to grow new specimens with greater genetic diversity than the current clones in the Gardens. With collecting banned in the Nature Reserve, the arborists hope to gather seeds from other populations farther west. The stop has been worthwhile, though, as the group are now aware of the species' wild form. 'The bark of the *Zelkova* is distinctive – mottled orange and stripy,' says Kevin. 'But the *Zelkova* in Georgia look completely different to the ones at Kew.'

From Babaneuri, the five continue north to Birkiani on the Alazani River and follow the Batsava tributary up into the foothills of the Greater Caucasus, travelling through a sparsely populated rural area of moist forests and occasional pastures. Here, their seed collecting begins in earnest. They harvest seeds from small trees and shrubs of black alder (*Alnus glutinosa* subspecies *barbata*), European hornbeam, rose species, common and Mediterranean medlar (*Mespilus germanica* and *Crataegus azarolus*, respectively) and Cornelian cherry, growing among grassland and at the edge of a woodland. The fruits of several of these species are harvested from the wild by rural Georgians for eating raw, for cooking and for making medical preparations. The arborists spend the night in Jokolo, south of Birkiani, which is a village of the

Kist people, a Chechen sub-ethnic group of Sunni Muslims. 'You do culturally see a difference in this mountain area; that's what makes these trips so interesting,' says Kevin.

As the arborists journey west, they frequently witness how the temperature and availability of moisture control the mix of arboreal species. At the village of Ghebi, for example, which lies roughly halfway between the Black and Caspian seas in the far north of Georgia, they observe how the vegetation changes with altitude from valley bottom to mountaintop. It's a similar story to when Henrik was driving the group up the hill to Zedazeni Monastery, except that this time the moisture gradient is reversed: it's wetter in the valley bottom and gets drier higher up. 'In the valley bottom below us, there's the river and there's obviously a lot of moisture available, so we see *Salix alba* [white willow], a very water-demanding plant growing there,' explains Kevin, as the group rests on the hillside overlooking where the Rioni River bisects Ghebi. 'Then there's some disturbance where you have the settlement beside the river and on the lower slopes, and you can see that the canopy is fragmented and there are some conifers. Then, higher up the slopes, there is thick forest, with oriental beech and oriental hornbeam, along with other species that are trying to outcompete each other through their ability to cope with dry soils.'

Over the next three weeks, the group samples seeds from trees and shrubs across the full range of Georgia's arboreal zones – from high in the mountains down to near sea level. The highest altitude they travel to is around 2,300 metres (7,546 feet), near the town of Akhaltsikhe in the south-western Samtskhe–Javakheti region where they gather seeds of the Balkan maple (*Acer heldreichii* subspecies *trautvetteri*) and the dwarf shrub Georgian snow rose (*Rhododendron caucasicum*) from disturbed alpine meadows and shrublands. Lower down, at an altitude of around 1,500 metres (4,921 feet) in the mountains around Shovi, they sample seeds of *Vaccinium arctostaphylos*, the Caucasian whortleberry, with its startlingly bright red leaves, as well as *Picea* and *Abies* near the Kutaisi-Alpana-Mamison Pass, close to Georgia's border with Russia. At this altitude, the cool and dry conditions suit conifers, their small needles having evolved to retain moisture, reduce wind resistance and photosynthesize all year round. Being in the branches of a *Picea* gives Tom a spectacular bird's-eye view of the Greater Caucasus. 'It was quite high and looked out over a valley with very dramatic scenery,' he recalls later. 'I was on a real high: there were so many cones and they were all covered in sap, and I was there for this one specific mission. I had climbed an *Abies*, which was taller than the *Picea* next to it and I'd swung from the *Abies* into the *Picea*, collected cones from the *Picea* and swung back. It was fun. A couple of cones have hundreds of seeds in and we got plenty. I came down with these big bags, saying, "Look what I've got!"'

Most of the seeds the arborists collect during their three-week adventure come from broadleaf trees, and are from the potential Goldilocks zone for Kew's future climate. These include oriental hornbeam from just north of Tbilisi, sweet chestnut *(Castanea sativa)* from near Borjomi, the coveted *Zelkova* from near Kataisi, Caucasian oak (*Quercus macranthera*) from south of Oni in the foothills of Khikhata mountain, and *Tilia dasystyla* from close to the mountain in the village of Bokva. Seeing the latter growing in the wild was a particular highlight for Kevin as it was among the limes included in his research and he'd previously only seen it growing in botanic gardens. And he was even more delighted to encounter the Pontine oak in its natural habitat. This species is ranked as globally endangered by the IUCN, and it only grows in the Lesser Caucasus of western Georgia and north-eastern Turkey, where its populations are decreasing. 'I'd read a lot about it and I really wanted to see it,' says Kevin. 'We didn't find it for hours; then I looked up and said, "Henrik, there it is – stop!", and we found it on a ridge. The trees were multi-stemmed, not massively tall but with really big leaves like a sweet chestnut coppice. It was incredible to see it; I never thought I'd get to see it in the wild. I was told by someone at the Oak Consortia that I would never find it in Georgia, so I took great pleasure in sending them a picture of one. There are not many people on this Earth who have seen that.'

The group had been helped in their mission to find the Pontine oak by fellow botanists in the area, who the British-Swedish team had been introduced to by Nukri and David at the IoB. The letter of introduction that the Georgians had provided in Tbilisi had also proved useful on several occasions, smoothing the way when locals were inquisitive about what the arborists were up to. On one occasion, when the group were looking for *Zelkova* trees at the edge of a timber yard, two farmers came across to see what they were doing. Tom recalls that the locals were initially stand-offish but after Nukri's letter was proffered and the word '*Zelkova*' mentioned, the non-English-speaking farmers immediately understood and took Henrik off to show him around the nearby woodland. After that, the locals brought out a bottle and invited the visitors to share with them a drink that Tom recalls was 'like a really strong port but dark pink, cloudy and pearlescent'. To this day, he doesn't know what it was. But the experience, and others like it during the expedition, confirms the importance of cross-border partnerships and collaboration in botany and wider science.

While Kevin, Tom and Sal are in Georgia, the spirit of networking and knowledge-sharing is strong back at Kew Gardens, too, where Rich, Will, Jamie and Cecily are holding the fort at Tree Gang HQ. In early October, as autumn continues its stealthy advance, two hundred or more delegates descend on the Gardens for a day of talks, tours and discussions on the future of horticulture. Here to participate in the Royal Parks Guild Apprenticeship Discovery Day entitled 'A Green Legacy: Growing the Future Together', around 140 of the attendees are either at apprentice level or are schoolchildren, beginning or considering their journeys into the horticultural or arboricultural world. The day is sponsored by the Tree Council, Kew, the National Trust and other institutions, with apprentices at this educational and inspirational event coming from Kew, the Royal Horticultural Society, the National Trust, Hampton Court Palace and the Commonwealth War Graves Commission, among others. These Discovery Days have been running for several years but this is only the second time that Kew has hosted the event.

As torrential rain gives way to just a persistent downpour, the first of three tour groups of 25 delegates assembles to meet Jamie for a tree tour with a difference. Although Jamie only gets round three old trees in this tour, he reveals not just their history but the secrets of how they are managed. For these remarkable trees have valuable lessons to teach us, and Jamie is keen to pass on their stories to this diverse group of people at a key stage of their careers. Ian Turner, from the Tree Council, a knowledgeable and friendly ambassador for tree management and tree planting, accompanies Jamie on the tours, adding to the fascinating discussions of healthy tree management here at Kew and beyond its walls.

Two of the trees that Jamie includes on his tour are among specimens that were imported from China in 1753 by nurseryman James Gordon and planted in the Gardens in 1762. Both of these 'Old Lions', have over the years been subjected to arboricultural treatments that are now considered outdated, which Jamie takes time to highlight. The first to come under his scrutiny is the ancient-looking Japanese pagoda tree near the Princess of Wales Conservatory, which has been reduced over the years to two recumbent remaining limbs of the once much larger tree. The other is the famous *Ginkgo biloba* or maidenhair tree. This specimen was originally planted next to the Great Stove – one of the first glasshouses at Kew, now long gone. As well as being an Old Lion, in 2002 it was named as one of 50 Great British Trees by the Tree Council for the late Queen Elizabeth II's Golden Jubilee. Ginkgos are extraordinary trees; this species dates back 25 million years and is more closely related to conifers than to broadleaf trees, despite its delicate fan-like leaves. The shape of these is similar to those of the maidenhair fern (*Adiantum pedatum*), which gives this tree its common English name, while the notch in the centre of the leaf is acknowledged in the Latin species name 'biloba'.

Jamie uses the stick end of his tour-group flag to point out to his listeners an unusual feature on the ginkgo's bark – a drooping nodule that makes it look as if the bark is almost starting to melt like candlewax. He takes delight in telling everyone these are 'chi-chis' – a name that comes from the Japanese word for breast. It's not certain why the tree produces these, although Harvard University botanist Peter Del Tredici thinks it might be a response to stress and that basal chi-chis can, in the right conditions, put out aerial shoots or adventitious roots, which can aid the tree's survival. They are only ever found on trees over 200 years old. Above the cheeky chi-chis, there is plenty more to see. Jamie shows the group the variety of different bracing systems that were installed by tree gangs past to aid the structural integrity of this precious old specimen – from older rigid ones made of steel wire to newer polyester ones with stretch. Such different systems reflect, again, how arboricultural knowledge has evolved.

Ian picks up the story: 'Today we try not to use bracing as we now understand that we need to allow the tree to move naturally and put on growth where it needs to in response to natural movement. We can reduce weight and mass to reduce the chances of limbs being lost, but if you make a tree rigid through bracing, you stop it from understanding the space it's in and from moving naturally. As we've evolved in arboriculture we've changed our thinking about braces, about using paints to cover wounds, about how to remove material or if to do that at all. In some ways we have an arrogance about what we think is best for a tree, without understanding fully its biology or ecology or whole life system,' he says.

Sometimes trees can teach arborists a thing or two, which becomes clear after Jamie leads the group to the huge dark green dome of the Turner's oak (*Quercus* x *turneri*) – a naturally hybridized semi-evergreen tree dating to 1798. Here, discussions move to soil health and aeration, for this tree is famous for inspiring a whole new way of managing the ground around tree roots. The soil quality at Kew is particularly poor: a sandy loam, often with plenty of gravel, and, in other places, peculiar areas of heavy clay where gardeners from previous generations brought in cart loads from elsewhere to try to improve the nutrients and water retention of the soil. 'The soil quality is so poor being here on the flood plain of the Thames,' says Jamie. 'You maybe only get 30cm of topsoil and then [it goes] straight into sand so it is very free-draining, and it dries out very easily. So, it is the last place in the country that you would probably choose to site a botanical garden.'

During the 1987 Great Storm, in which Kew lost more than 700 trees, the Turner's oak was hauled 25 centimetres out of this feeble substrate by the strong winds and then resettled back into the ground. Previously it had been struggling and even started to die back but having had the soil around its roots de-compacted by the force of nature, it took on a whole new lease of life. Tony Kirkham, who was then in charge of the Arboretum, realized the significance of this event, and began to use a tool called Terravent (at the time used to aerate sports pitches) around other trees to simulate the action of the storm. The storm and this subsequent response sparked a whole new era of understanding and managing compaction around the roots of trees in public spaces. Jamie explains to the group how today at Kew the Tree Gang use 'air spades' and 'geo-injectors' to pump air into and fracture the compacted ground beneath trees, and to introduce biochar and clay into the sandy soil. This not only adds nutrients to the soil but improves its physical structure. After such treatment, the area under the canopy of each tree is mulched, which also helps to enhance soil health – and, crucially, deters visitors from walking beneath the branches and further compacting the soil.

Since the Turner's oak inspired a new way of viewing the ground beneath its wide, spreading branches, decompaction methods have been used on many specimen trees at Kew. Jamie and the team have noticed that trees previously seen to be suffering have really benefited from soil remediation work. 'Although my job is climbing around in the canopies of trees, much of tree health happens down in the soil,' he concludes. Ian agrees: 'Yes, long-term it is all about maintaining soil health,' he says. 'We can get as technical as you like – using microscopy and genetic sampling of the soil – but we need to make sure we are not using chemicals, that we're increasing organic matter, managing people and footfall around trees, and we need to understand what's going on in the soil. For example, do we have a healthy fungi-to-bacteria balance? It's not just about what nutrients are there, but also about the structure of the soil, we need to make sure we have the right information and detail before we make decisions,' he explains. 'We need to encourage "bioturbation" [movement of the soil by plants and animals, such as worms] and let nature do what it does best, we don't necessarily need expensive tools or products, but we need to be inquisitive, and we need to be better communicators about the new knowledge we are learning about tree health.' Aiding a tree's natural health is clearly the message of the day – a vital lesson Jamie has enjoyed sharing through Kew's precious heritage trees, his enthusiasm not dampened by the rain. He didn't even put his hood up.

Kew has the practice of sustainably increasing organic matter in the Gardens' soil down to a fine art. Any pruned or fallen timber is normally taken to a large holding bay in the centre of the Stable Yard near the Lake. This yard has long been the hub of arboricultural activities at Kew and, of course, was once home to the horses that helped with all of the jobs on-site – from mowing to moving fallen timber. The workshop that the Tree Gang operate from still has signs of its past life as a Victorian stable block, including an old tack rack on one wall. Today, though, all green and woody waste is brought to the Stable Yard by tractor and trailer (or in big black skips) and deposited in large piles in a designated area to await shredding.

Here, a process begins that means that materials are recycled in a completely natural and sustainable way to contribute back to the health of the living collections.

The large open area at the centre of the Stable Yard is more than it seems, comprising a purpose-built impermeable concrete pad that is surrounded by a bund to contain any liquid run-off, and concrete barriers to retain the segregated material. Green waste is pre-sorted into piles of either woody or herbaceous material and deposited in the yard in separate areas. But of course these materials cannot make great compost on their own. To aid the creation of the enormous amounts of mulch that the Gardens need – and with Kew's own horses now long gone – a delivery of around 50 cubic metres of stable bedding from Hyde Park Barracks arrives every week. The barracks, situated in Knightsbridge in central London, is home to the horses of the Household Cavalry Mounted Regiment – the King's official bodyguard who can often be seen practising drills on Horse Guards Parade. Even the composting at the Royal Botanic Gardens, Kew is a royal affair.

Both woody and soft green organic materials are inspected for any 'hazardous' or inappropriate waste that shouldn't be part of the composting process before any mixing of materials begins. Herbaceous material is blended with the stable manure on a 1:1 ratio, while in a separate process woody materials are added to the manure on a 3:1 ratio and then put through a 20mm trammel screener. Both the 'soft mulch' and the woody mulch are then spread into their own windrows to begin the maturation process, which lasts for approximately two weeks. After that, the windrows are monitored and turned weekly using a vehicle called a telescopic loading shovel. Dan McCarthy, Logistics Manager for the Stable Yard, who is in charge of this process with a team of four others, reveals that the soft mulch can rot down and be ready in as little as nine to ten weeks, while the woody mulch can take up to twelve weeks. During this time, a dark brown liquid called leachate can often be seen seeping out and away from the piles (especially if it has been raining) but this is captured and pumped into a holding tank underneath the concrete yard. 'The windrows are monitored for temperature and moisture content daily,' says Dan, 'then if needed, they're watered using the leachate through a weep hose.' Dan is keen to point out that this is often done at night or at weekends to avoid staff having to put up with the smell!

Dan explains that it's important to keep the moisture and temperature in the windrows at optimum levels in order to create the best mulch possible. It's a closed-system process that's always in motion, with materials frequently coming in and out of the yard. In autumn, the area is busy with tractors loading up trailers full of mature mulch to take out into the Gardens. The woody mulch is used as a weed suppressant around trees, while the soft mulch is used as a soil conditioner and to add nutrients to a range of different planted areas. In total Dan estimates that Kew makes 3,500 tonnes of composted mulch every year. It's a product that is as local as it comes and for which the ingredients are perfectly controlled.

Across the autumn and winter months, Kew's gardeners will be working hard, spreading this dark gold across the ground, aiding the life and activity within the soil, and keeping it healthy. It can particularly help the mycorrhizal fungi that grow through the soil, their network of hyphae linking with a tree's roots in a mutual symbiosis. Such fungi supply extra water and nutrients to the tree while, in return, the tree supplies sugars it has made through photosynthesis. The fungi extend the reach of the tree's roots as it searches for food and can even connect it to other trees.

But there is one other job that the compost can miraculously perform while it is still in the yard, and that is to cook anything placed inside it. The heat generated inside the windrows can reach 75°C, as fungi and bacteria break down the materials, and on cold mornings the piles steam gently. To make use of this natural heat, it's been known for the gardeners, as well as members of the Tree Gang, to try cooking baked potatoes inside the windrows (fully wrapped in tin foil of course) – a perfect treat for a cold autumnal day.

Any large trunks of fallen trees that are too large to compost are kept to one side to be reused for timber products. In early November, the trunk and large branches of two Hungarian oaks (*Quercus frainetto*) are collected by staff from the Quarter Sawn mill in Edale. They carefully transform the enormous pieces of timber into usable sections ready for making into household products. This work will be undertaken by a company that Kew has a new partnership with called Selwyn House, which specializes in making high-end products from British-grown timber. These include everything from chopping boards, candle sticks and butter knives to small pieces of furniture. So far, as well as the Hungarian oaks, some birch, box, a Greek fir (*Abies cephalonica*) and a western red cedar (*Thuja plicata*) have also been hauled away to be given a second life. Wanting to reuse the timber in this way is part of Kew's whole sustainability ethos to try to reduce all waste and reuse what it can to benefit the Gardens. In this way, former prize botanical specimens will be transformed into goods on display in the Gardens' shops, enabling visitors to take home a unique piece of Kew history.

Visitors strolling around the Gardens in mid-October encounter a startling scene on Riverside Walk, near Kew's western edge. Close to the base of a tall London plane lies a skeleton, face down, arms and legs splayed, against a backdrop of fallen autumn leaves. Two more skeletons are propped up at the base, their skulls and ribs penetrated by a tangle of white plastic tubes that snake their way across the ground and upwards into the tree's highest branches, lending the camouflaged trunk a striped appearance. Every few minutes, a pulse of red illuminates three parallel tubes on the trunk, while others flash blue, yellow and green. In the first case of its kind at Kew, the elegant London plane has gone rogue and begun sucking the blood from the bodies of anyone close. 'This is the carnivorous tree,' explains Tom, but there's no cause for alarm. This is actually part of the new Kew Halloween trail. Since returning from Georgia, Tom has been working with the team to install the programmable neon light tubes that are a key part of the new seasonal exhibit. 'We've installed 45 reels, each 12 metres long, and the main contractor installed another 25 reels. It's about 200,000 LED lights in all.'

Kew's first Halloween trail is slowly being brought to life – or perhaps drained of it – by the event's curators Raymond Gubbay Limited and Culture Creative. Close to the carnivorous tree, groups of illuminated pumpkins with maniacal grins are clustered in hay carts and on the ground, forming the Gardens' first 'living-dead' collections. Terrifying Dementor-like ghouls stalk visitors strolling amid the trees. And giant spiders with fat black-and-white-striped legs patrol the grass, near where a sign warns: 'Beware of the monsters'. On this cool, overcast day, with the scent of mulch and fallen leaves pervading the breeze, the developing scene already lends the Gardens a spooky feel. But once the trail officially opens in a few days' time, visitors will be able to up the 'fright level', if they wish, by choosing to come during specially arranged twilight or moonlight opening hours. The idea is that the darker it gets, the spookier it gets. Some may even stumble across a headless horseman.

For now, though, there's still work to be done installing lights on the large Turkey oak (*Quercus cerris*) near the Children's Garden, which is to feature in the Halloween trail prior to making its usual glittering appearance in the regular and much-loved Christmas at Kew event that will open in November. For this, the Tree Gang again assist the event curators by undertaking tasks that require working at height. This includes completely illuminating the Turkey oak from the base of the trunk up to the smallest of branches, as well as hanging long 'neon' tubes of LEDs in the cedars along Raffill's Walk – connecting the Temperate House to the Marianne North and Shirley Sherwood galleries – and between the Treetop Walkway and the Lake Crossing. Transforming the oak into what the Tree Gang refer to as the 'pea-light tree' is particularly painstaking work, which takes three weeks to complete. Creating the dazzling display requires at least three arborists to be on-site – two up in the canopy wrapping five-metre lengths of small lights around the trunk and every branch and stem, and one on the ground, passing up (via ropes) cables, lights, electrical connectors and any tools the aerial workers may need. The lights are stapled to the tree, which may sound drastic but doesn't harm the oak as it has very thick bark.

An annual October event on the Tree Gang's calendar (Christmas has long come early for them), it can be a treat for the climbing arborists, affording them the pleasure of being high in the oak's canopy, without the physical demands of wielding heavy chainsaws. 'The first year that I was properly involved in doing the pea-light tree specifically, I remember being right at the top of it on this cold, slightly windy, drizzly day, swinging around in the tree in the wind and seeing across London, and then looking down and seeing my colleagues and thinking that I'm really lucky to be paid to be doing this,' says Jamie. 'Frequently, you just get to the top, do your work and then come down. I think that at that moment I realized how lucky I was. It's a job in which you're using your skills and you are also having a nice time with your colleagues and at the end of it you get an amazing display.' Cecily agrees: 'I really enjoy Christmas at Kew because it's such a lovely thing to do and to bring your family to. Because you can't really show your family what you do every day but when they see a whole tree lit from root to tip it's so nice.'

Today, Tom and Rich are up in the tree, working to dress smaller branches on their own, and passing lights between them to wrap the larger ones. The tinny clicking of their staplers beats out the rhythm of the work. Will is ably assisting from below, frequently refilling the staplers passed down to him on a rope before sending them skywards again. Navigating the tree using ropes and ladders, Tom and Rich carefully place the strings of LEDs in equidistant rows about ten centimetres apart, from the canopy down to the ground. Placing each strip of lights, and figuring out how the tree will be viewed from every angle by visitors, is pure creativity at height. The logistics of working out exactly how to do this efficiently while making sure that everything is connected properly is mentally tiring. And the fact that the main body of the tree is to be dressed in bright white lights, with its extremities in green, further complicates matters. 'The best way to do it is to start from the tip with a five-metre strip [of green lights] and come in [towards the trunk] and then attach it to white lights,' says Rich. 'You can connect them with wire connectors so you have two [lengths] coming into one but we often come into a union and then do a wide-spaced wrap out and then follow it back in the gaps, so we don't use the wire connectors. You end up with a string of 32 five-metre lengths and then you terminate it and bring it down to the bottom.'

In mid-November, Christmas at Kew opens. For the next six weeks, a nightly procession of visitors spends two or so hours wending its way around the illuminated trail: kicking up holographic snowflakes on the Broad Walk, spotting leaping fireball fish and passing under mist arches at the Lake Crossing; watching flowing waves of light illuminating the Temperate House and rocking along to the falsetto tones and rock riffs of 'Christmas Time' by The Darkness in the spectacular

Palm House finale. And then, as the trail comes to an end, they get to see the most magical part of all (or so the Tree Gang would have them believe) – the pea-light adorned Turkey oak, its every twig and branch glittering in bright white and green against the pitch black sky. The success of the event, in its 12th year, is in no small part due to the expertise of the Tree Gang and other teams in balancing the use of the living collections for entertainment with keeping them healthy and safe as an invaluable scientific, horticultural and historic resource.

The need to strike this balance has long presented a challenge for those in charge at Kew. In fact, Kew's first director Sir William Hooker faced that issue as soon as he began work in 1841. The government would have liked Kew to have been another park full of gaudy Victorian flower beds but Hooker and others fought to also make it into a place of scientific importance, building on the living collections already in place. Hooker had to strike a balance between attracting and satisfying an increasing number of visitors each year, and keeping the growing number of rare and beautiful plants safe for education and research. He dearly wanted to do both, stating both objectives in his very first annual report on the Gardens. Successive directors faced calls for longer opening hours, for cafés and restaurants, prettier areas and flowers, and to allow picnics. Since it opened to the public, Kew has been enjoyed in many different ways, from plant-based festivals to art and music in the Gardens, but its prime purpose has always been about conveying the importance and beauty of plants to all – whatever form that may take. The plants will always take precedence, but encouraging visitors to appreciate and enjoy plant diversity in different ways, rather than see them simply as green wallpaper, is an important mission too.

At the southern tip of the Gardens, alongside the stunning collections of the Pinetum, sits a unique area of Kew, where visitors can appreciate trees in a wilder setting. This is known as the Natural Area or, alternatively, as the Queen's Cottage Grounds. This latter, older name refers to Queen Charlotte whose *cottage orné* still nestles in the middle of the woods here, where once the Georgian royal family had picnics and admired a small menagerie kept there. It was Queen Victoria, however, who ceded these 15 hectares (37 acres) to Kew in 1898. By that time this area had become a wilderness due to lack of maintenance, but as Kew historian Ray Desmond reveals: 'It was a condition of the gift that this area should remain in its present natural state ... to preserve its "great sylvan beauty"'. The grounds were first opened to the public in 1899 when extra bluebells and native daffodils were planted. Adding native species and clearing away non-natives is a practice that has continued since that date (for example 150 oaks, birches and poplars were planted in 1914 and another 35 oaks added in 1984) but more recently this area has become a focus for the conservation of much rarer native trees, including subspecies of whitebeam (*Sorbus aria*) and the Plymouth pear (*Pyrus cordata*).

Today the Natural Area is managed by Natural Habitats Supervisor Ruth Brookes, who is part of the wider Arboretum team. Ruth sees this area as 'a functional ecosystem rather than a collection – a showcase for UK woodland ecology'. Indeed, the contrast is palpable as visitors cross from the formal Gardens into the Natural Area. Rustic sweet chestnut fencing appears, there is a large stag beetle loggery left to go wild, and decaying trees remain standing, their tops cut into jagged crowns to attract more insects. And of course, once April and May arrive again, the ground among the trees will be carpeted with English bluebells and wild garlic just as fresh lime-green leaves begin to appear on the trees, creating a delight for the senses as well as the bees and other pollinators. Having this small woodland at Kew offers a whole new set of opportunities and challenges for working with trees in a different way. Here they must be managed to maximize biodiversity and the aim is to keep the wood ecologically healthy.

Ruth has been working with the Tree Gang on a number of projects, particularly drawing on their climbing and technical skills. Recently they have been helping with the 'veteranization' of non-native species such as Turkey oaks. Veteranization involves prematurely ageing a tree by, for example, adding bird-nesting holes or slits under the bark for bat roosts, or even inoculating it with fungal spores. This ageing of the tree encourages a wider range of habitats and food for a plethora of invertebrates, birds and bats. Ruth prefers to artificially age these non-native species rather than asking the Tree Gang to remove them entirely. Although quite small, the Natural Area has to be seen as part of a bigger geographical and ecological picture. 'This area is one of a number of reservoir habitats,' Ruth explains. 'There are so many old parkland trees and habitats in south-west London [that form part of a wildlife corridor].'

Ruth (who uses they/their pronouns) was previously a ranger for the National Trust's Lanhydrock Park in Cornwall, conserving nearly 1,000 acres of woodland and grassland.

With their habitat management experience, Ruth brings a whole new vital set of skills to nurturing this area of Kew in the best interests of its ecology. They want to encourage all manner of native species here by creating a variety of habitats from scrapes, ponds, and long and short grass areas to dead hedges. As part of that mission, Ruth is working with Sal and the team at the Arboretum Nursery to plant black poplars (*Populus nigra* subspecies *betulifolia*) here. This is Britain's rarest native hardwood tree, with only 7,000 individuals left. Black poplars were once a fundamental part of the UK landscape – even appearing as the background treescape, alongside elms, to John Constable's 1821 painting *The Hay Wain*. They were once valuable timber trees, used for making carts, buildings, clogs and even arrows. Today, however, they are only known in small, fragmented populations across the country, as their preferred riverside and floodplain habitat has given way to agricultural improvements, housing and industry.

'People won't be that familiar with this tree and its distinctive dark bark and curved trunk,' says Ruth. Identification is made more complex by the many similar hybrids and cultivars of poplars that are out there. But people living close to Kew, in Barnes, may have more chance than most of recognizing the trees, as an elderly population of wild black poplars grows there next to the Thames towpath. This is a remarkable relict population with impressive genetic diversity and a good mixture of male and female trees. The presence of females is treasured as only 600 are thought to exist in the UK out of the 7,000 total. Ruth's work at Kew alongside Sal in the Arboretum Nursery has been to nurture and plant new saplings in the Natural Area, created from cuttings taken from the Barnes population. This vital work is contributing to a much wider local collaboration that is part of Richmond Borough's Biodiversity Action Plan being carried out in conjunction with the Friends of Barnes Common and expert conservation arborist Jamie Simpson. It was through Jamie's DNA fingerprinting of black poplars across the country that the value of the Barnes population was revealed, and the conservation of this species set in motion.

Cuttings taken by conservationist Jamie and Kew's Head of Arboretum Temperate Collections Tony Hall in recent years are now growing in the Natural Area, the Arboretum Nursery and in the project nursery at Barnes. This work is building on previous projects by the Forestry Commission and Royal Parks (at Richmond Park) and Wakehurst's UK National Tree Seed Project, to help the species. While the Barnes nursery is supplying the majority of saplings for planting up new populations of black poplar along the Kew, Richmond and Hampton Court sections of the Thames towpath, Ruth and Sal are focused on making sure that they have enough of the right clones to expand Kew's own population as part of this vital conservation effort. Each successful sapling must be labelled with the date of the cutting, planting and, importantly, the tag number of the distinct clone it was taken from, alongside any other pertinent information, to make sure it contributes to future viable genetically mixed populations. If a sapling dies, Ruth aims to replace it with the same clone to ensure that the genetic diversity at Kew is maintained.

Kew has had black poplars since at least the 1970s, as its oldest specimens here date from then. Personal papers of the former Kew Herbarium curator Edgar Milne-Redhead in Kew's Archives show that he was measuring black poplars at Kew in the 1960s and 1970s, and encouraged many others to plant black poplars then too. 'Some are genetically distinct,' explains Ruth. 'We have a tree that we call the "Kew clone", but we're not entirely sure where it came from originally,' they continue, highlighting the need for good record-keeping. Ruth hopes that having such distinctive specimens may aid the species' resilience in the face of climate change. They have been surprised by just how tough the black poplars, old and new, are at Kew, which seem to have been little affected by the 2022 drought or recent deluges of rain. Ruth tours the younger specimens in the Natural Area regularly, checking on their growth – 'they grow very quickly, around a foot a year,' Ruth confirms – ensuring that their labels with their clone numbers are intact, and making sure brambles and invasive alliums aren't impinging on the area cleared for them to grow in. Ruth is also looking for new sites that may be good spots for a few of the nine saplings currently growing in the Arboretum Nursery, which they intend to plant this winter with team member Beckham Cant and a dedicated crew of enthusiastic Kew volunteers. Meanwhile, Sal is already planning to take cuttings from those new recruits before they are planted out to ensure Kew has back-up plants. Once in, the new black poplars will join the vibrant sylvan ecosystem that thrives alongside the more cosseted tree and shrub collections nearby, and which offers a very distinct experience to those who make their way down to this unique woodland.

In line with the Landscape Succession Plan, Kevin is planning to emulate the wilder look of the Natural Area across other parts of the Gardens, albeit in a more managed and curated way. He plans to use the seeds from Georgia to start developing layered plantings that are both more visually interesting and sustainable for the future. For example, in the Pinetum, where Kew's conifers are currently concentrated, the idea will be to mix in some broadleaf species to create a patchwork of contrasting and eye-catching textures and colours. 'We need more diversity in there because the conifer collection is at extreme risk under future climate-change scenarios,' says Kevin. 'So, by building in those broadleaves, if we do lose a tree there's not going to be such an impact on the landscape. We'll use a lot of the things like *Acer tataricum*, *Carpinus orientalis* and *Carpinus betulus* that we collected on the Georgia trip. If you imagine the Pinetum now, you have the grass layer, then stems – and then the canopy is really high. We collected [seeds from] these trees in dense woodlands where they were growing as understorey. So, we're going to plant them as understorey [here at Kew] to provide different layers. This will be the methodology we will use throughout the Arboretum going forward.'

Before this work can get under way, however, Kevin needs to solve a puzzle: where exactly are the seeds? Before leaving Tbilisi, Kevin and Henrik had been to the Plant House to obtain permission to send the seeds to Gothenburg Botanical

Garden, with the idea that Henrik would then send on to London the seeds destined for Kew. This had seemed an easier option when in Georgia than obtaining separate sets of permissions to ship the seeds to the two locations directly from Georgia. But by late November the precious package has still not arrived from Sweden.

    Seeds can generally be classified into two types: orthodox and recalcitrant. Orthodox seeds are those that can tolerate drying and tend to remain viable even if they start to desiccate. Many plants from arid areas have evolved to have orthodox seeds, as drying out is an occupational hazard for them. Scientists at Kew's MSB use this characteristic to their advantage by drying seeds to around 3 to 7 per cent moisture content (on a fresh weight basis), thereafter storing them for posterity at temperatures of -20°C. Many seeds kept in this way can still germinate years or decades later. Recalcitrant seeds are trickier to conserve for future use as they cannot be dried and banked in the same way; scientists are still trying to develop satisfactory methods for preserving them in a way that retains their viability. While, in nature, orthodox seeds might lay dormant until sufficient moisture is available to support their growth, recalcitrant ones, having evolved to anticipate a ready supply of water, often germinate straight after being dispersed.

Most of the seeds collected in Georgia are orthodox, as the trees from which they were collected, such as hornbeams, beeches and limes, naturally grow in relatively arid steppe conditions. Those of the oaks, maples and birches, however, are recalcitrant. While the orthodox seeds will most likely be able to cope with the postal delay, the fear is that the recalcitrant ones may either dry too much to be viable or might start to grow in their packaging in transit. It's a worrying time for Kevin, Tom and Sal as they eagerly await news of the seeds' arrival.

Eventually, after several weeks, the parcel turns up and is rushed straight to the Arboretum Nursery for Sal to process. With the seeds having been sorted and cleaned by the group while in Georgia, those of each species are already packaged in dedicated paper envelopes labelled with the plant's Latin name. In the Nursery, the seeds are subsequently counted and weighed, and this information added to the envelope. One envelope declares its contents to be 339 common pear (*Pyrus communis*) seeds, weighing a total of 12g; another encloses 203 seeds of the ivory-flowered bladdernut (*Staphylea colchica*) seeds, together weighing 100g. Sal logs all the relevant data onto a spreadsheet: the species name, the fact that it's naturally sourced, the country of origin; the collection number (each collection from a separate site in that country has a separate number); and more.

With all the necessary information recorded, Sal conducts a sink test for those species with only small collections by putting the seeds in jars of water: those that are healthy and likely to germinate will sink, while those that are compromised are more likely to float. Seeds of various colours and sizes representing *Fagus, Cornus, Euonymus, Crataegus, Abies, Acer* and *Quercus* species are soon being tested in this way. Of the 58 endangered and recalcitrant *Quercus pontica* acorns collected, only two sink. The trees had already dropped their acorns when the group encountered them, so these seeds were collected from the ground, increasing the likelihood of their having already dried out or been infested. Sal plants the two sinkers straight away, but because the tree is so rare and 'I can't bear to throw them away', she also plants all the other seeds. To ensure that any pest is contained, the pots are covered with plastic and sealed. In time, Sal hopes it may be possible to micropropagate clones of the endangered oak using plant-tissue culture techniques. She also plants up seeds of recalcitrant *Q. macranthera*; these acorns were collected from the tree and have a good chance of thriving.

In her work, Sal also often uses a 'cut test' to determine the likely viability of seeds. The test involves cutting either five or ten of the seeds of a collection to see whether, as hoped, they are full and healthy, or, as is sometimes the case, infested or empty. This is particularly useful for determining the likely germination rate of tree seeds collected in the Gardens, which are often grown up to saplings and then used as grafting stock. Some trees have a 'mast' year every few years, in which they produce a bumper crop of seeds; however, often many of these are empty. Performing the cut test can help to save time and resources being used to try to grow such 'duff' seeds. As part of Sal's role is to supervise two students who have come to gain experience within the Arboretum Nursery, she uses some of the seeds of the Balkan maple (*Acer heldreichii*) from the Georgia trip to demonstrate the cut test. Of the ten she cuts, only one is not viable, indicating that a good proportion of the seeds will probably germinate. She decides not to perform a cut test for most of the Georgian species, however, not wanting to waste seed from these hard-gained, wild-sourced prize collections.

Because the seeds did not arrive until cold autumn weather had already set in, Sal decides to put most of the remaining seeds into 'cold stratification'. This involves placing the seeds in a fridge, in plastic bags with some moist vermiculite-containing 'Kew mix', to mimic the conditions of the Georgian winter season. They will stay here at temperatures of around 2°C until spring, when they will be potted up ready for germination in the warmer weather. For some species, such as *Carpinus*, *Cornus*, *Ilex* and *Tilia*, Sal will subject them to warm stratification first, at 18–21°C. This is to start the process of breaking their dormancy. If they germinate, she'll pot them up; if not, they'll join the others in the fridge. As Sal packages up the seeds that are going into cold stratification, she notices that some already in the fridge have started growing: these are *Tilia tomentosa*, which were collected on the Romania trip a year before. Within the Kew mix, thin white radicles – embryonic roots – have wormed their way out from the grey-brown seeds. As the limes have decided to germinate early, Sal will plant them up alongside some young *T. tomentosa* plants that she potted up last autumn and that are already growing well in the Nursery.

The Nursery, a large glasshouse located across the Stable Yard a short walk from the Tree Gang's workshop, comprises six computer-controlled zones. The warmest of these is Zone 1, which is where many Kew trees and woody shrubs begin their life, as either seeds or cuttings. Heated benches here help seeds to germinate, while the combination of the heated substrate and cooler air ensures that cuttings put their initial energy into developing strong roots rather than growing new leaves. Tents are currently used to maintain the level of humidity required for different species. Adjacent to Zone 1 is the slightly cooler Zone 2, to where young woody plants are moved after becoming established and from where they progress to Zone 3 for hardening off. Grow lights are available in Zone 4; this zone, together with Zones 5 and 6, are where herbaceous and Mediterranean plants requiring higher light levels are located. At the front of the Nursery, is a laboratory-like area that Sal terms 'the potting shed'. This is where Sal and her team carry out much of their planting work, applying cutting-edge technology to coax the Arboretum's future trees to life. Visitors can view the work going on here from a dedicated entrance and viewing gallery in the Pinetum near the Lake.

'I supervise everything in the Nursery,' explains Sal. 'We've got two members of staff and we've usually got two students. So, I set the timetable for the week for what we've got to be doing. I'm also the main trainer for the two new members of staff so I'm training five days a week at the moment – because it's very hands-on and I need to share that information. Between 7.30am and 10am, everybody focuses on their own zones. The priority is always watering. Everybody's allocated a zone, particularly the students. And whether the students are studying at apprentice or diploma level it's expected that they'll become more autonomous as their placement – which is usually about three months – goes on. At the beginning of their placement they will have a look at all the jobs that need doing and put them on the board noting whether they're important or urgent – so they're learning how to manage the collection.'

Notable in the Nursery collection today, alongside rows of salvia and ferns destined for the Salvia Border and Woodland Glade, and surplus camellias and rhododendrons from Wakehurst, are the trees important to both Kevin's research and the Landscape Succession Plan that have been grown from seeds collected on the Romania expedition. In Zone 1, with five or six seedlings planted to a pot, are the aforementioned *T. tomentosa*. Standing on red-tinged stems, five or so centimetres above their grey-gravel substrate, the seedlings' flamboyant five-lobed cotyledons – embryonic leaves – are now being succeeded by the species' more conservative 'true' leaves. Meanwhile, outside in a poly tunnel, are the 20cm-high saplings of *Fagus* x *taurica*, now dressed in copper-coloured leaves that seem too big for the plants' diminutive stature. 'Also from the Romanian collection that germinated last year are the European hornbeam and the oriental hornbeam,' says Sal.

'Kev is going to be looking at the eastern one to see if it has more drought tolerance than the western one.'

For Kevin, the seed-collecting trips to Romania and Georgia have helped to visually validate the time and passion he's put into his research. For a start, the expeditions clearly demonstrated to him how similar the conditions in summer are at Kew to those of the steppe, confirming the power of his modelling approach. He's impatient now for the young trees in the Nursery to grow, so they can be planted out in the Gardens and, he hopes, draw on their in-built drought tolerance to thrive in the future heat. 'It was amazing to look at those environments – and look at what Kew is like in the summer – and find it's so well matched,' he says. 'The grass here is all brown, it's all dry free-draining soils, and it's exactly the same as the models predicted and where we were collecting from. From that point of view it was incredible to see. It was great to do the research but to actually see it – I learned a lot. It gives you more confidence in your work and to say, yes we are going down the right way.'

For now, though, climate change is rearing its head in other ways, driving extreme weather exemplified by Storm Bert, the second UK named storm of the season. This is the first named storm to affect Kew this year (the earlier Storm Ashley having battered more northerly and westerly locations). When the Tree Gang tours the Gardens in Bert's aftermath in late November, they find that the storm has toppled a specimen of *Eucalyptus parvula* in the Children's Garden. One of only two specimens of this species in the Gardens, this eucalypt is commonly known as the Kybean or small-leaved gum (*parvula* means small). It is native to New South Wales in Australia, where it only grows across a small, limited range west of the Wadbilliga National Park and Glenbog State Forest, which lie south of Canberra, and where it is listed as endangered by the state government, and under threat from agriculture and land clearing. The IUCN Red List of Threatened Species regards the population as stable although severely fragmented. In the UK it is highly valued for its beautiful peeling bark and fragrant soft blue-grey foliage, and for being one of the more cold-hardy of these Australian endemic trees.

Although wind speeds did not get above 45mph near London during Storm Bert, the direction and force of the gusts were too much for this tree, with its twisted long limbs. But, at around 60 years old, it had done well; this species rarely grows for more than 70 years even in the best conditions in the wild. That the fallen specimen is contained inside the tall hedges and gates of the Children's Garden is something of a blessing, as the area is easy to close. However, the tree presents an immediate hazard so the Tree Gang must remove it as quickly and safely as possible. As they arrive to make their assessment, the eucalyptus presents a sorry sight: its smooth, V-shaped trunk, striped in shades of brown and grey, lies twisted over on its side, exposing its roots. One substantial stem lies along the ground, a pale split recording its point of impact. The other arches away from the ground, reaching three metres or so in the air. Tom and Jamie begin by fencing off a wide area around the tree with red and yellow warning tape. 'We'll nibble away at the small branches and make a bit of space for us to work in and then we'll drop the top part of the trunk down,' says Tom, knowing in an instant the best approach to take.

The high-pitched whirr of an electric chainsaw starts up and Tom starts to slice quickly through thin branches at shoulder height. Jamie then drags the detached branches, still bushy with twigs and leaves, across a path, past a water fountain and over a small wooden bridge to where the wood chipper stands 20 metres away. Here, Cecily feeds the wood into the machine. Close to the tree are wooden playhouses and other climbing equipment that would usually be busy with children playing. Once the accessible smaller branches have been removed, Tom takes a long-barred petrol chainsaw to

Rich and Tom work methodically together over several days to wrap a Turkey oak (*Quercus cerris*) from roots to branch tips in small 'pea lights', to create a glittering spectacle for Halloween and Christmas at Kew.

The Stable Yard is the centre of a huge compost-making operation, creating around 3,500 tonnes of composted mulch every year.

Left to right: Henrik Sjöman and Emil Wallin from Gothenburg Botanical Garden, and Kew's Kevin Martin, Tom Fry and Sal Demain, visit Tbilisi National Park, Georgia, at the start of their seed-collecting trip.

The Tree Gang and colleagues encounter oriental beech *(Fagus orientalis)* trees growing in a gully in woodland in Tbilisi National Park, Georgia.

Sal Demain inspects the seed from an oriental beech *(Fagus orientalis)*. Close inspection reveals small holes drilled by weevils.

A managed landscape near Gudauri in the Greater Caucasus mountains of Georgia, incorporating housing, grazing pastures and woodland.

A species of pine tree near Bakuriani, Georgia. During their three-week seed-collecting mission to the country, the Tree Gang gathered seeds from a range of evergreen and deciduous trees.

A view from southern Georgia in the Lesser Caucasus range looking across the central valley to the snow-dusted Greater Caucasus in the north. The two ranges host diverse habitats that are home to 6,400 species.

Mature *Abies nordmanniana* cones being collected by Tom from 24 metres (80 foot) up a tree looking over the Chanchakhi River on Georgia's northern border with Russia and the disputed territory of South Ossetia.

Above left *Tilia tomentosa* seeds collected in Romania in 2023 have germinated, representing a new generation of trees that will hopefully prove resilient to the changing climate at Kew.

Above Some of Kevin, Tom and Sal's precious collections from Georgia – including these *Zelkova carpinifolia* seeds – are put into cold stratification in the Arboretum Nursery ready for sowing in spring.

Above left The Arboretum Nursery, under the care of Arboretum Nursery Supervisor Sal Demain, is home to a huge range of plants being grown for the Arboretum, Natural Area, and more ornamental parts of Kew, such as the Woodland Glade.

Left Seeds collected by Kevin, Tom and Sal in Georgia undergo a 'sink test' to see which are still viable after their long trip to the UK via Sweden.

Above The old *Ginkgo biloba* at Kew was planted in 1762 as part of the original royal arboretum and is one of the Gardens' venerable 'Old Lions'.

Left The Wollemi pine *(Wollemia nobilis)* from Australia is extremely rare in the wild but has been conserved through mass propagation. Kew was used to trial its hardiness in the UK before it went on general sale.

Opposite page top This large tree transplanter was invented by William Barron (1805–1891) in the mid-19th century. Kew first bought one in 1866, which soon became known as 'the Devil' by the gardeners.

Opposite page bottom In winter, the bare forms of deciduous trees in the Arboretum are revealed. Here, swamp cypresses *(Taxodium distichum)* on an island in the Lake offer beautiful reflections.

In spring the Natural Area around Queen Charlotte's Cottage is carpeted with English bluebells as the trees begin to unfurl their fresh new leaves.

The oak *(Quercus)* collection at Kew is one of the largest in the world, with 149 taxa represented. The English oak *(Q. robur)* (seen here) is known for its value for wildlife; jointly, *Q. robur* and the sessile oak *(Q. petraea)* have been found to support over 2,300 species.

the airborne stem, close to where it branches from the trunk base near the ground. He cuts a wedge in the lower side and then slices down from the top, cream sawdust streaming from the blade. There's a splitting sound, and the upper stem drops a foot or so onto the lower one. Tom then methodically cuts this curved wood into thick segments, which has the effect of lowering it to the ground, slice by slice. Each time, he drives the blade down from the top, then hammers in a metal wedge to open up the slit so the chainsaw bar can penetrate deeper. Inside, the timber is salmon pink.

The team works rapidly, clearing away additional smaller branches as they come into reach and leaving larger sections of timber where they fall. Their industry keeps them warm against the late November chill. With half the curved upper trunk brought down, the remaining part rises from the ground like the Loch Ness Monster from its lake. Tom slices through the lower part of the 'neck' but the arch stays put. He gives the base segment a hefty push, then steps quickly away as the timber section falls away and the trunk drops once more. When the rest of the arched stem has been similarly lowered, Tom begins to cut away the branches attached to it, now conveniently just below shoulder height. Above, thin clouds filter the sun in the pale blue sky. By the time the team leave to get a coffee, the trunk has been reduced to a series of cylindrical segments on a carpet of woodchip; just the canopy remains to be tackled. The space left behind opens light up to the floor, and gives breathing space to the neighbouring tree, another eucalyptus.

Today's clear weather is short-lived; within a couple of weeks, extratropical cyclone Storm Darragh hits south-east England. It fells eight more trees across the Gardens, including a *Picea schrenkiana* near the Lake Crossing, the only specimen of the Canary Islands juniper (*Juniperus cedrus*) – a critically endangered species – and a *Paulownia fargesii* in the Woodland Glade. Thankfully, the latter, at least, has already had its seed collected and its progeny are now growing in the Arboretum Nursery. The loss of all of these scientifically valuable specimens is a reminder that nothing is permanent in the landscape. No matter how carefully the Tree Gang look after the Arboretum, it responds naturally to the environmental pressures placed upon it.

Part Four

WINTER

Kew Gardens is the most biodiverse place on Earth. Its 130-hectare (320-acre) site hosts 16,900 species, making it the Guinness World Record Holder for the largest collection of living plants at a single-site botanic garden. As such, there are few better places for trainee horticulturalists and arborists to learn about the world's plants. Students enrolled for a range of Kew qualifications therefore participate in regular plant-identification tours as part of their courses. During each tour they are shown plants exhibiting interesting characteristics at that time of the year, on which they are later tested. Over the course of their studies, students build up a thorough knowledge of temperate and tropical flora through the Gardens' living collections. It's one reason why Kew graduates are much sought-after by botanic gardens around the world and an example of why such collections – including the Arboretum – are so important.

Since starting his combined Kew Arborist Apprenticeship and Level 2 Arboriculture qualification in October 2023 – making him a temporary member of the Tree Gang – Arthur

Gregg has been taking plant-identification tests every month. Today, on a cold, damp afternoon, he joins a group of ten other Kew students at the north side of the Mediterranean Garden for an identification tour focused on plants of 'winter interest'. With Christmas at Kew in full swing after dark in early winter, fewer visitors tend to explore the Gardens in the daytime. But for those who do — and who can resist the lure of the warm, steamy, tropical Palm House — there is a surprising amount to see. For a start, those hankering after a more traditional Christmas experience can observe profusions of mistletoe growing on hawthorn (*Crataegus*) along Thorn Avenue, south of the Temperate House. And red and yellow berries abound on the hollies of Holly Walk, the path that in the early 18th century was called 'Love Lane', separating Prince Frederick's Kew estate from his monarch parents' Richmond estate.

The plant-identification tour begins, however, with two plants that today lend an exotic look to many gardens across the UK: the Chusan palm (*Trachycarpus fortunei*), native to parts of China, Japan and Myanmar, and the dwarf fan palm (*Chamaerops humilis*), which hails from the west and central parts of the Mediterranean. Both are hardy evergreens and look in fine fettle, their spiky leaves strikingly silhouetted against the pale grey sky. Jake Davies-Robertson, a supervisor in the Arboretum who is leading the tour, pulls a large leaf of the Chusan palm from a black bucket of pre-picked stalks, twigs and leaves, and passes it around the students. He explains that, although the leaves of both palms look similar, this *Trachycarpus* leaf has a smooth petiole (leaf stalk), while that of the *Chamaerops* is spiny. As the students walk a short way to where both plants are growing, Jake points out the fibrous material on the Chusan palm's trunk, which he says is woven into rope in Japan for tying fence panels.

The next two plants Jake gives the students to scrutinize both have glossy leaves and distinctive white flowers. The leaves of the paper plant (*Fatsia japonica*) are large, with palm-like lobes, against which its pom-pom-like spherical flowers clearly stand out. The fragrant leaves of the Chilean myrtle (*Luma apiculata*), by comparison, are small and oval, while its flowers have four waxy petals and long stamens. Students who take time to find the plant later in the Duke's Garden will find that the woody shrub also has striking cinnamon-coloured bark that peels to leave white and orange patches. 'Remember the plants may have black berries by the time you do your identification test,' warns Jake. The test, in which students are given cuttings of the plants to identify in the classroom, won't take place for another few weeks. While this gives them time to familiarize themselves with different specimens of the plants in the Gardens, they need to be mindful of how the plants' life cycles may have moved on since seeing specimens on the tour.

Several of the plants that Jake has chosen to show the students are particularly fragrant, such as the curry plant (*Escallonia illinita*) – which smells like its name. 'It's a real scratch and sniff,' he says as he hands round a rust-coloured twig with small, leathery, toothed leaves on it, and explains that the volatile oils in its leaves are responsible for its scent. 'There's one that smells incredible right now at the south end of the Princess of Wales glasshouse,' he says. Also strongly scented is the wintersweet or Japanese allspice (*Chimonanthus praecox*), which has highly fragrant yellow flowers that beguile the students. 'It smells citrussy,' declares Arthur, holding a sprig to his nose, shutting his eyes and breathing deeply. 'It smells like soap,' concludes another student.

After discussing eight or so species, Jake walks the group up to King William's Temple at the apex of the Mediterranean Garden and then down steps to arrive at a gnarly-looking cork oak (*Quercus suber*). The bark of this tree, 'one of many, many oaks', says Jake, yields the cork we find in wine bottles. For this, the outer layer of bark is prised off but the inner cambium (needed by the tree to distribute water and nutrients around its structure) remains intact. This process can be carried out every ten years for two centuries without harming the tree, since it can regenerate its bark, making the cork industry highly sustainable. But, as winemakers have switched to using plastic corks, large swatches of former productive cork oak forests have been abandoned or cleared, affecting water tables, soils and economies. Conservation programmes are under way in south-west Europe and north-west Africa – where *Q. suber* is a native species – to conserve cork forests and promote sustainable livelihoods.

From the Mediterranean Garden, the group trails Jake down Cherry Walk to the Temperate House and then turns left to arrive at the new Winter Garden, created in 2022. Located on a small mound, the Garden is landscaped with plants that have evolved to be able to cope with the frost, reduced sunlight and limited opportunities for pollination that come with the British winter. One such tough plant is *Mahonia nitens* 'Cabaret', with glossy and spiny dark green leaves. It has orangey-red flower spikes in autumn, which, Jake explains ruefully, 'are over but they're really nice'. Close by, the students examine *Skimmia* x *confusa* 'Kew Green', a shade-loving evergreen shrub, with pale green buds in winter that open to white flowers in spring.

On leaving the Winter Garden, the group heads south,

past the Shirley Sherwood and Marianne North Galleries and under the Ruined Arch, where the students encounter a large evergreen bush to the left of the path. This is *Camellia japonica* 'Kingyo-tsubaki', the cultivar name of which translates to 'goldfish'. It was so named when developed in Japan in the 18th century because of its unusual evergreen leaves that divide into three at the tips, a little like a fishtail. Growing very close by is a robust tangle of white-stemmed brambles, the Latin name of which – *Rubus cockburnianus* – draws giggles as the students attempt, badly, to pronounce it. The stems are, in fact, purple but have an attractive white bloom on them.

The final two plants that the students examine are both trees. The first, *Polylepis australis*, from northern Argentina, has reddish, heavily peeling bark that looks like filo pastry left in the oven too long. The second, the tanbark oak (*Notholithocarpus densiflorus*), has strange acorn-like seeds, the cups of which appear frilly, like a ballerina's tutu. Despite its common name, this is not a true oak, although it is in the same family (Fagaceae). 'It has very tough, leathery leaves,' says Jake. 'It's got to survive the Californian heat.' The species doesn't seem to mind the cold either though, having been grown at Kew since 1874.

Having now examined the tour's quota of 20 plants, the

students disperse. In the coming weeks they will need to examine the photos they've all been snapping during the course of the tour, and visit different specimens in the Gardens to ensure they are well acquainted with the plants by the day of the test. Some of today's selected species have similar characteristics that could trip up a student who is ill-prepared. 'We have to go into the School of Horticulture, and in the lab they'll have put cuttings of each of the plants – nothing else – on the table. Then you'll be asked, "What is number nine?" and there'll be a twig then you have to go, "Oh is that an English oak?"', explains Arthur. 'You have to give the name in Latin, with the family, the genus and the species. I think some of the higher-up students are asked more things, like where the plant is from and a bit more in-depth information but for our course we just have to give the name.'

Arthur grew up not far from Kew in Whitton in west London. He didn't enjoy school and was unsure what to do for a career. He recalls how, one day, a man who was working in a tree, jumped down beside where he and his friends were sitting, and proceeded to tell them about what being a tree surgeon involved. Arthur was fascinated. He went on to work in construction for a couple of years, including working at height on roofs, but knew at that point that his passion was working with trees. 'I applied for a couple of apprenticeships through the gov.com website and got interviews for both of them, so then I applied for the apprenticeship at Kew,' he says. 'My parents had been members for donkeys' years and I used to come here to Climbers and Creepers when I was a little lad so I knew the place well. I applied not expecting anything at all – not even expecting a message back – and I got given an interview. I was really excited, so I did my interview and in it you had to climb a tree – which went really well – and I got the job. I was so happy with myself.'

The plant identification tests form part of Arthur's Kew Arborist Apprenticeship, which also involves him undertaking practical work with the Tree Gang, keeping journals of this work, and making labelled collections of garden weeds. He gets one day every fortnight off from Kew to study for his Level 2 Arboriculture qualification, which requires him to attend lectures and practical sessions at Berkshire College of Agriculture in Maidenhead, part of the Windsor Forest Colleges Group. Gaining the Level 2 qualification calls for study of wide-ranging aspects of arboriculture, from the health and safety needs of the job, using equipment safely and carrying out tree work using appropriate equipment, to understanding the benefits of trees to humanity, the principles of establishing, growing and caring for them, and problems arising from pests and diseases. Of particular relevance to being an apprentice at Kew, Arthur's college work is also teaching him the importance of identifying trees and the value of using the scientific names.

As winter progresses, other members of the Tree Gang also get the chance to learn some new skills. One cold, crisp morning, Arthur, Will, Tom and Kevin, as well as Arboretum supervisor Jake Davies-Robertson, gather beside a black pine close to the Pagoda and Japanese Gateway to find out more about how light detection and ranging – or LiDAR as it is better known – can be used in arboriculture. Senior Research Leader Justin Moat and Research Assistant Isabel Openshaw, who both work in Kew's Spatial Analysis and Data Science team, plan to use LiDAR to scan the pine to generate a three-dimensional image of it and at the same time explain to the group how the technology works. Just as sonar and radar use sound waves and radio waves, respectively, to map objects, so LiDAR scanning uses light sent out from a laser to digitally render objects. In this way, the technology is able to generate a three-dimensional model of a building, or, more interestingly for the present group, an individual tree or entire woodland.

'Once you've built these 3D virtual environments you can then start working with them and carry out simulations or modelling,' explains Justin. 'For example, you can put the tree into a virtual wind model and add your landscape to it – and ask, "What happens to my trees when I put this sort of wind across this landscape? How will it change the shape and movement of my trees?" We've also started to see people using it for virtual tree surgery before they do the work. You can look at the scan of the tree and see how it's balanced, and where its centre of gravity is. Then you can virtually start chopping limbs off to see how that changes the tree, how it changes its centre of gravity. And I suppose you could do that for aesthetic reasons too, to see how it might look after tree-surgery work.'

The black pine has been chosen as the subject for today's scan as it is to be cut down. It is leaning slightly, and, despite having some green growth, many of its needles are rust red. In comparison to the holly oak (*Quercus ilex*) that the pine stands beside – the luxuriant, dark canopy of which almost extends down to the ground – it seems sickly and low on vigour. Tom and Kevin have deduced that the pine has needle blight that will gradually weaken it, which is why it must be removed. However, its life will not have been in vain as it will contribute to scientific research after its death. Specifically, it will help to enhance understanding around the amount of carbon held in tree biomass, critical if humanity is to bolster absorption of carbon from the atmosphere to try to stabilize the global climate.

Once the tree has been scanned, Justin and Isabel aim to use the resulting 3D digital image to deduce the tree's volume and then employ that figure to calculate its likely carbon content. They will also obtain estimates for the carbon content of black pine that have been made using allometric equations to calculate tree volume. This approach, which is widely used by the forestry sector, involves taking a particular measurement – such as trunk diameter at chest height – and using a mathematical formula for the species in question to deduce the size of the whole tree from this measurement. When the scanned pine is cut down, they hope to weigh it to generate an accurate figure for the tree's carbon content, against which they can compare the equivalent results obtained from the scan and the allometric equations. In doing so, they hope to show that LiDAR scanning is more accurate than using allometric equations in calculating the carbon content of tree biomass, and to confirm the validity of their methodology. Although LiDAR is expensive, and therefore unlikely to replace the use of allometric equations, it could provide a way of understanding the level of uncertainty inherent in the results, ultimately improving the accuracy of the method.

'By scanning the tree it allows us to get a 3D model of what it actually looks like and then we can break that 3D model up on the computer into all of the components and virtually weigh the tree – and then we'll get a much closer estimate of the true volume for the tree compared to the allometric equations,' explains Justin. 'Nature is highly variable. Think about an oak tree in the middle of a field with lots of space and think of one in a forest squeezed together with other trees; the two are completely and utterly different in shape and biomass because of the way they have been growing. So allometric equations fall apart quite quickly, especially with big trees. We'll be able to compare the scanning and the mathematical methods to the results from weighing the black pine and see which is most accurate.'

Justin and Isabel set up a large scanner that they have brought with them about five metres from the base of the pine. Standing on a sturdy aluminium tripod, the columnar LiDAR unit has the scanning hardware, a GPS and processing capabilities built in, and a camera on top. It only requires scans from three positions around the tree to capture a full three-dimensional image, but Isabel and Justin plan to make as many as eight to be on the safe side. 'It doesn't take long,' says Isabel as she stands the scanner in its first position and sets it at a 90° angle for it to make its first vertical scan. The top cylinder of the machine slowly rotates as it scans the ailing tree with light emitted from an inclined mirror-like window. It uses near-infrared light to capture the image, as these wavelengths reflect strongly off vegetation. Once this scan is complete, Isabel rotates the scanner to horizontal and repeats the process. Over the course of 30 or so minutes, she moves the heavy tripod in three-metre increments around the tree until she's back to the starting location.

For each scan, the GPS records the position of the scan on the ground, while the internal computer calculates – using the speed of light – the time taken for pulses of light emitted from the scanner to strike and return from the trunk, branch and leaf surfaces. Once uploaded to a computer, generated data appears as a 'point cloud' from which any material that isn't part of the tree needs to be identified and removed. 'On one occasion the light beams hit a seagull so there was a beautiful outline of a bird,' says Justin. 'So, we remove all that and "segment" the image to identify parts that we don't want to work on, such as the ground, and isolate the specific tree that we do want to work on.'

Once this process has been undertaken, student Mathilda Digby who is undertaking her PhD with Kew, will divide the tree into 'pipe cylinders' – akin to actually cutting it up *in situ* into logs – and use these to calculate its volume in cubic metres. This figure will then be used to determine the amount of biomass in the tree (essentially its volume without water) and this, in turn, will yield a figure for the amount of carbon stored within it. Once this calculation has been made by the scientists, all that will remain is for the Tree Gang to cut the pine down, weighing it as they go. With Christmas fast approaching, however, that will happen next year.

On the last day of work before Christmas, the Tree Gang get to finish work early and attend the Arboretum's annual Christmas barbecue. But before they can do so, they need to make safe an oak tree growing in the Natural Area. Earlier in the year, when the 100-year-old *Quercus robur* in question was in leaf, Tom had spotted that three of its branches had no foliage and were dead. They need to be removed because the dead wood is overhanging a path. Because the oak is in the Natural Area, however, Tom wants to do so in a way that will encourage biodiversity to populate the tree. Instead of simply slicing off the branches with a chainsaw, therefore, the Gang will use a winch to rip the dead wood from the tree. Tearing the timber in this way will create a jagged wound, replicating the effect of a dead branch naturally falling from the tree, and produce crevices that act as ready-made roosting sites for bats, and habitats for insects such as saproxylic beetles.

Tom, Will, Cecily, Jamie and Arthur are taking part in this tricky operation. The three dead branches they plan to remove all stem from one of the five or so main branches of the 19-metre-high oak. They plan to attach a rope to each branch in turn and use a hand-operated Tirfor winch to put increasing pressure on the rope until the timber fails and the branch is ripped from the tree. As with all jobs that the Tree Gang do, a dedicated risk assessment must be carried out. Today, Will has been allocated this task, which he fulfils by completing a pre-prepared Kew form. First, he describes the site and the nature of the job, as well as detailing the weather conditions – cold but sunny. Next, he outlines the hazards and dangers that are present or may be present, arriving at an initial hazard rating of 'high'. From here, Will considers actions that can be taken to reduce this risk – such as using signage to deter visitors from entering the area, wearing proper clothing and so on. This helps him to arrive at the 'residual risk rating', which he determines is 'medium'.

'The reason we're not taking it down to a 'low' is because we're using a winch-cable-strop system, which can potentially be very dangerous,' he explains. 'If anything snaps, you can get a cable whipping past your head at 90 miles an hour, so there are rules as to how close you can get to the "cone of death" when you're winching. I've therefore added the caveat "cannot further reduce the risk". "Medium" or "low" is acceptable; "high" is not acceptable. If it comes out as residually high you have to go away and rethink the job.'

With the risk assessment completed, Tom uses the Big Shot catapult to fire the throw line into position over the first branch they mean to remove. Arthur ties on a hefty 20mm blue rope to the line, which, as Tom pulls on the line, curls up out of the black bucket containing it. A bowline knot is then run up the rope; this stops at a fork in the branch, lassoing it tight. Tom places a metre-long metal winch some 35 metres from the oak, wrapping a thick black webbing sling around the solid trunk of another tree to secure it. He places a protective mat between the sling and the bark and uses a pin to attach the two ends of the sling – capable of holding a weight of four tonnes – to the winch. Back at the oak, Jamie connects the rope to one end of a thick steel cable that is coiled up in a tyre. Cecily then rolls the tyre backwards away from the oak towards the winch, uncurling the cable as she goes. On reaching the winch, she feeds the cable into it and secures a lock that grips it. Then she attaches a long handle to a bar on the winch and pushes it towards the tree – which has the effect of pulling the cable through the winch.

Now it's time to take up the slack, which Cecily starts to do, pumping the winch handle. The others watch and wait as the cable slowly tightens. While thin, grey clouds speed across the sky, sporadic sunshine lights up the amber oak leaves layered on the ground. The cable tightens with each click of the ratchet. A Virgin Atlantic plane roars across the sky, bound for nearby Heathrow Airport. Cecily continues to work the winch, but the branch remains firmly attached. Finally, after several tense minutes, there's a loud crack and a forked branch crashes to the ground. The branch, which has split in two on impact, is clearly dead. Its bark is covered in velvet green moss and grey-blue lichen; the end that until a few seconds ago attached it to the tree, is jagged and split. All five of the Gang roll the larger part of the branch to one side of the path, then Will and Arthur remove and slice up the rest of the wood and stack it up on the other side.

As Rich is currently on shared parental leave, Arthur has been taking on an increasing share of the Tree Gang's workload. The 'work experience' part of his Kew Apprenticeship had initially got off to a slow start after he'd broken his wrist in spring this year. However, he'd continued to attend his college sessions and once he was able to, began learning on the job with the Tree Gang. To start with, this involved mostly simple tasks, such as dragging wood to the chipper, and clearing the site and making it safe. Then, once his wrist healed, he began undertaking chainsaw work, and, finally, he was able to climb trees. 'It's a very team-orientated job,' he explains. 'We're not off doing our own things across the site, we're all working together and communicating together, and you are kind of thrown in the deep end. You have to be part of the team from day one and the stuff that you do on day one you will still be doing in 30 years' time; you'll also have other jobs to do but you will still basically be picking up bits of wood and putting them in the wood chipper.'

Today, the wood chipper is nowhere to be seen, though, as Ruth Brookes is keen for dead wood to be left in the Natural Area. Therefore, the branches will all simply be tidied up and left to rot and form new habitats *in situ*. With the first branch cleared, it's time to tackle the second. This time, everyone takes a turn with the Big Shot, each aiming to fire the beanbag-weighted throw line up high around the second branch. After a few unsuccessful attempts, it is Tom who fires the line into place, delighted at having done so in front of the others on his first attempt. Then the winching process begins again, this time with Jamie and Tom tightening the cable. Will and Arthur stay with them, while Cecily keeps her eyes on the branch from a safe distance. A few minutes pass, as the cable tightens once more. Then, as the tree emits a few sharp cracking sounds, sending screeching parakeets into the sky, Cecily alerts the rest of the Gang on their intercom system. 'It's hard to know if the cracking is coming from the branch that's being broken off or not,' she says. More cracks sound and the lassoed branch wobbles. Then, in spectacular fashion it shatters into pieces. 'Whoooaa,' shouts Cecily. 'It's like it exploded!'

As before, the Tree Gang machine rolls into operation to clear the wood before they tackle the final branch. This time, the whole of the main stem comes away from the tree, splitting into two as it falls. It means that all the dead wood has now gone from the oak. The team clear away the wood once more before packing up. Barring any major incidents requiring their immediate attention over the holidays, their work is done for the year. As they head back to the workshop, the smell of meat cooking on the barbecue beside the Arboretum Headquarters wafts across the Stable Yard.

By the time the Gang return in January, the Arboretum's evergreen trees are taking centre stage, the deciduous ones having retreated into their skeletal winter form. The magnificent blue-green atlas cedars *(Cedrus atlantica)* are standing to attention beside the Broad Walk. The big cone pine (*Pinus coulteri*) growing near to the Elizabeth Gate is living up to its name, displaying fabulously spiky cones that can be big as 50 centimetres long and give the species the nickname of 'widow-maker'. And, the pair of Wollemi pines near the Orangery are proving resilient to the British mid-winter cold. But the main attraction when it comes to evergreens at Kew is, of course, the Pinetum. Spread across the southern end of the Arboretum this is a dedicated collection of conifers, which includes pines, firs, spruces and cypresses. Planted over 16 hectares (40 acres), the Pinetum skirts one side of the Lake and continues round eastwards alongside the Natural Area heading towards the Pagoda. This is a special part of the Gardens, with a quiet beguiling atmosphere all of its own.

The collections here are incredibly diverse – and include some endangered species – but the Pinetum was once even larger. This area was first designed and planted as a conifer collection by Director Joseph Hooker from 1871. But this was not the first pinetum at Kew – it fact it was the third. The first was part of the original royal arboretum that occupied two hectares (five acres) of ground next to the Orangery. A list of plants collated in 1813 known as the *Hortus kewensis* shows that Kew had an impressive 56 different conifers at this time. The second pinetum was planted in 18 hectares (45 acres) of new land around the Palm House in the 1840s as part of William Hooker's expansion of Kew as a new public botanic garden. Here, you can still see some towering, beautiful conifers today, such as stone pines, *Pinus ponderosa*, *P. pinaster* and deodar cedars.

Joseph Hooker's new pinetum was ambitious. He wanted to plant every conifer hardy to Britain, arranged in family groups for ease of scientific comparison. It was part of a taxonomic and aesthetic reorganization of the whole Arboretum under his watchful eye. Joseph moved some conifers that had been planted by his father from elsewhere in the Gardens and brought new species in until he had amassed around 1,200 specimens. He arranged these by family, as planned, but also with 'New' and 'Old World' species facing each other across pathways. Conifers were extremely fashionable in the late

19th century so a pinetum was a welcome new attraction for visitors, but Joseph was also fascinated by conifers himself. In 1860 he had visited Syria to study the Cedar of Lebanon (*Cedrus libani*), and in 1877 he would head to North America to research some of the native conifers there too.

Joseph had delighted in both the new landscaping and the additions to the Gardens. Kew historian Ray Desmond conjectured that it was a welcome relief from all the correspondence and administration of his new directorship, and that he revelled in being outdoors. Indeed, Joseph wrote to his friend the naturalist Charles Darwin in 1868: 'I am getting very proud of the Gardens, in which I really have worked tremendously hard for two years.' Joseph and his curator John Smith also laid out seven avenues of conifers radiating from the Pagoda at this time, including those of juniper, Irish yew and Japanese cypress. Although these are no longer present, junipers are still to be found in the old heather garden next to the Pagoda.

In 1908, William Jackson Bean recommended that visitors enter the Pinetum via the Lake-side path, where they would be welcomed by several monkey puzzles (*Araucaria araucana*) from Chile. From here they would pass hemlocks (*Tsuga*) from North America and Japan, firs and then spruces (*Picea*), after which they would encounter a large area of pines (*Pinus*). Taking a path eastward towards Lion Gate then led the visitor through yews, podocarps from Australasia, *Torreya* and *Cephalotaxus* from California and Japan, umbrella pines (*Sciadopitys*), *Cryptomeria*, redwoods (*Sequoia*) – 'the greatest tree wonders in the world' as Bean called them – and then cypresses and *Thuja*, before reaching the larches (*Larix*) and Larch Walk. Parallel to this route was Cedar Vista – a grassed processional vista lined with an avenue of blue-tinged Atlantic cedars (*Cedrus atlantica*) with the Pagoda as its central focal point. Many of the trees that Joseph Hooker planted, with additions from Bean and Dallimore, still stand today.

However, in 1908 Bean was bemoaning the state of the Pinetum. It was suffering terribly from London air pollution, and soot clung to the trunks and branches of the conifers in such quantities that he said anyone who had to work with them came away looking like a chimney sweep. Even then, summer droughts had a detrimental effect, especially on the moisture-loving firs and spruces in Kew's readily draining soils.

The air pollution, and issues with water and soil, eventually led Kew to look elsewhere to establish a complete conifer collection for the nation. By 1924 Bean and new director Arthur Hill had settled on a site in Bedgebury, Kent, which was owned by the Forestry Commission. Bean and Dallimore laid out a design for what would become the most complete conifer collection in the world and, from early 1925, Dallimore and a small group of men began planting. An extraordinary few decades followed of gathering species and specimens from Kew, nurseries, other renowned gardens and collectors until Bedgebury became firmly established. Throughout the whole of its formation, William Dallimore oversaw every detail, continuing in a curatorial role even after he retired from Kew. Today, Bedgebury remains pre-eminent. Solely run by the Forestry Commission since 1965, it still has strong ties to Kew today.

Although Kew's own Pinetum is now home to a smaller version of its original collection, there are some spectacular arboreal highlights. In the Redwood Grove is Kew's tallest tree – the coastal redwood (*Sequoia sempervirens*) from California, which stands at 40 metres. There are also dawn redwoods from China (*Metasequoia glyptostroboides*), a species thought to be extinct and known only from the Cretaceous fossil record (dating back to 145–66 million years ago) until being 'discovered' alive and well in China in 1943. Locally, this species was known as *Shuǐshān* or water fir. Kew's first specimen was planted soon after in 1948. The Wollemi pine, with its similar story, can be seen growing on the islands in the Lake. Endemic to Australia, it became a global horticultural sensation in 1994 after a local ranger came across it in a remote canyon in the Blue Mountains. Both species have been saved through mass propagation and being planted in botanic gardens around the world, as well as being sold to the public. In this way the wild specimens have been sheltered from the greedy eyes of avid plant collectors who would otherwise have sought them out and taken them from the wild. There are many other trees to look out for in the Pinetum, some of which are endangered in the wild, including the Japanese Douglas-fir (*Pseudotsuga japonica*).

According to the IUCN, of the known 615 species of conifers in the world, 34 per cent (or 211) are threatened with extinction. This makes any work to conserve species and their genetic diversity incredibly important. Kew's work with partners in the UK and overseas ensures that Kew's specimens can aid future conservation efforts. Such was the case with the 'critically endangered' Koyama's spruce (*Picea koyamae*) from Central Honshu in Japan, where less than a thousand individuals now grow. Threatened by logging as well as natural disasters such as typhoons, its future looked uncertain. It was first introduced to Kew in 1915 by British 'plant hunter'

Ernest Wilson who was funded by the Arnold Arboretum in Boston, USA. Almost a hundred years later, in 2013, Kevin also successfully collected seeds in Japan, working with Japanese partners and the International Conifer Conservation Programme run by Royal Botanic Garden Edinburgh. Today, a new selection of these rare trees is growing in Kew's Pinetum as an *ex-situ* conservation population.

Another rare species that has found sanctuary in the Pinetum is the Polish larch (*Larix decidua* var. *polonica*), of which Kew only has one mature specimen. This species is endemic to Poland where it still grows in scattered forests in the Western Carpathians. According to the IUCN, it is endangered, and almost extinct, in the wild. Lately, Sal has propagated several saplings in the Arboretum Nursery from the seeds of the mature Kew specimen, of which two have been planted along Larch Walk. Today, Tom and Arthur are to plant another. The pair are holding the fort while the rest of the Tree Gang are busy with other tasks: Cecily is in Serbia with Kew's Tom Freeth and Gothenburg Botanical Garden's Henrik Sjöman, forging new alliances for potential future seed-collecting trips; Kevin is at Hillier Nursery; Rich is still on shared parental leave; and

Will is attending a perfumery course elsewhere at Kew. While larger tasks would not be safe with just two arborists, one thing that they can easily complete alone, especially at this time of year, is some tree planting.

Weatherwise, it's the perfect day for it. The seemingly endless leaden grey skies of January have finally passed, and February brings with it some cold bright days with golden sunlight playing across the lawns – Tom's favourite kind of weather. Snowdrops and winter aconites are appearing all over the Gardens, while the spidery flowers of the witch hazels are just passing their best. On Larch Walk – a formal avenue of different species of *Larix* – the clusters of bright lime-green needles and scarlet ruffled flowers, so indicative of spring, are yet to appear on these deciduous conifers. The Walk offers a formal entrance to the Pinetum and the Natural Area: an elegant gateway into this very different part of the Arboretum. But halfway along it there is a gap between the trees created by the loss of a European larch (*Larix decidua*) over a year ago, and it needs to be filled to keep the avenue looking complete. It's the perfect spot for another Polish larch.

As the sun tries to bring some warmth to the air, Tom and Arthur drive out in the Kubota buggy pulling a trailer piled high with a variety of tools ready for any eventuality they might encounter, as well as a small pile of freshly made mulch. They stop at the obvious gap in the avenue. The small tree that will make its home among these tall sentinels is today only about one metre high, similar in stature to the two other saplings that are now beginning to find their roots on the other side of the pathway. All three will grow up in the shadow of their parent tree, which still stands about 20 metres away. That original has 'HNRY' and '1922' on its label, meaning it was donated by the famous plantsman, botanist and author Augustine Henry (1857–1930) in 1922.

Henry is best known for his introductions of, and expert knowledge about Chinese plants (he even has quite a few named after him, including a lime that features among those Kevin is researching: *Tilia henryana*). Henry's expertise stemmed from the travels he undertook in China while working for the Imperial Chinese Maritime Customs Service, and he saw many stunning botanical sights there. He was not just active in China, however, and his interest in temperate shrubs and trees reached across the world. Henry also donated another of the larches on this avenue, so this is now becoming a place to honour a man who donated more than 500 plant species to Kew and many thousands of herbarium specimens too. Indeed, in 1935, J W Besant, Keeper at the National

Botanic Gardens at Glasnevin in Ireland, claimed: 'The wealth of beautiful trees and flowering shrubs which adorn gardens in all temperate parts of the world today is due in a great measure to the pioneer work of the late Professor Henry.'

Planting a tree at Kew is not a 'dig a hole and stick it in' scenario, as the Gardens have set standards for tree planting that are rigorously maintained. Such standards are based on scientifically trialled experiments in tree growing that give any tree the best chance of reaching its full potential at Kew. They also celebrate how aesthetics and consistency are important when planting a tree here at this UNESCO World Heritage Site.

As this Polish larch sapling is another special addition to the avenue, Tom and Arthur intend to plant it with due care. They take time to make sure the planting spot is just right – equidistant between the current trees. A bamboo cane then marks the spot while they retrieve two semi-circular boards, half-moon lawn-edgers and turf-lifting spades (with wide flat heads like pizza paddles) from the trailer. The two boards when placed together are multi-functional – they create a 1.5-metre-diameter doughnut shape, provide a board for standing on to avoid squashing the grass outside of the circle, and also form an inner circle for the tree to be planted in. The outer edge is a guide for Tom and Arthur to use with the half-moon lawn-edgers to create the wide planting space. They work together, standing on the boards, to cut a circle in the turf, then move the boards off and lift a thin layer of turf out into a waiting trug. Placing the boards back onto the soil allows them to see exactly where the perfectly central planting hole needs to go.

In recent times it had become standard advice to dig a square hole for a tree, as it was thought that planting trees grown in circular pots into circular holes didn't encourage roots to grow outwards into the surrounding soil. However, trials of growing trees in all manner of different-shaped holes – even star shapes – revealed that the shape of the planting hole in fact bore no relation to the successful establishment of the tree. Gardeners also used to dig huge holes for small trees to go into, but it has been found that digging a hole more in keeping with the size of the pot it has grown in is much better for its establishment – otherwise it sits in a sea of loose soil with little to anchor itself to. Another key thing that has made a difference to better establishment is the pot the tree is grown in, and this larch has come in an 'air-pot' – an odd, black, spiky-looking thing now used by most professional growers. This five-litre air-pot (they can be made to any size needed and are reusable) has holes all up the sides to allow good soil aeration and drainage, and works to prevent the roots circling around the inside of the pot. This gives the tree a better chance of putting down fresh roots in its new home.

Tom and Arthur begin to dig a hole – just one spade's depth, to match the height of the pot – but they quickly and literally hit a problem. A large root is right in the middle of the hole they want to create. To ensure it is a dead root and not one from a nearby living tree, Tom carefully scrapes away the outer bark of the root and then pulls up Google Street View on his phone. It has an old image of Larch Walk on it that shows where the old tree used to be – and sure enough it used to grow pretty much where he is standing. He's happy that the root once belonged to the old tree, so Arthur retreats to the workshop to find some tools big enough to tackle the issue. They thought they had prepared for every eventuality but bringing an axe to a planting hole wasn't on their list.

With the aid of both a mattock and an axe, the root comes away and Tom is relieved to get final confirmation that it was indeed a dead piece of wood. Once gone, it is easy to see the quality of the soil here – an extremely sandy loam – which offers a very free-draining substrate for these trees to grow in. This is not something many trees like, but the larches seem to be managing so far. The pair don't add any extra compost to the hole as they want to encourage the tree to get its roots out into the soil as soon as possible. They firm the soil at the base of the hole and place the tree in to check that it will sit at the correct level – that the top of the pot soil is not being buried under the normal level of the ground. This task is aided by a long red piece of wood with a central point marked on it, which they lie across the hole. Taking time now to make these checks – that the tree is central and perfectly level – means that this sapling won't have to be moved again.

Once they're both happy, Tom unpeels the air-pot from the root ball, gives the plant a quick prune and places the tree in the ground. The loose soil is replaced and firmed in after every few spadefuls until the hole is perfectly full and level. The ground is raked and then those handy boards come out again. Placing these back around the tree now allows Tom to see where four stakes need to go to make them perfectly equidistant from the tree and each other and also parallel with the path. Every detail is being considered. Once knocked in, these posts are the sturdy foundation for a green barrier cage to be placed in a circle around the new tree, which will help protect it from mowers, people and wildlife. Even the ties used to attach this miniature fencing are placed at designated heights so that when anyone looks at new trees at Kew, they all look consistently presented. Tom explains that attaching a stake to the tree itself is unnecessary as the aim is to plant the trees when they are small enough to get their roots down quickly. This also helps them to put on tension wood where needed to react to prevailing winds and weather. Finally, the soil inside and outside the cage is mulched with glorious black, wonderfully pungent compost from the Stable Yard, which will add nutrients to the soil and keep moisture in to give this little larch a good start in life.

As they clear away the tools and make sure the area is free of debris, Tom reveals that this is the first tree he and Arthur have planted together. Hopefully, it's a memorable one, as it has added to both the cultural and conservation significance of the Arboretum collection. All that is now left to do is to ask Tom Freeth's team for a new permanent label for the tree, which will be put in a place by a volunteer. The Polish larch will then have fully joined the ranks in this arboreal processional avenue.

Planting trees at Kew has a long history of course, but not all were planted by hand. One piece of historic engineering that once helped plant many of the trees in the Arboretum is still in existence in the Stable Yard. This is the Barron's tree transplanter. This enormous Victorian machine is the remarkable achievement of the landscape gardener William Barron (1805–1891) and was designed to make the lifting, moving and transplanting of large trees an easier task. Barron was by no means the first to invent such a machine – he followed in the footsteps of Lancelot 'Capability' Brown, James McNab of Royal Botanic Garden Edinburgh and others – but his versions proved particularly successful, and he was clever in their promotion. Barron's 'Large Machine' – of which Kew has the only known remaining example – is constructed of two huge oak beams that sit atop an open wooden structure with ropes, metal screw jacks and windlasses (to aid lifting a cradle placed under the root ball of a tree), and four enormous metal-banded wheels. The whole piece of machinery is designed to be taken apart, backed up around a tree by two or more heavy horses, put back together again and then used to winch up and carry a tree away to its new position – all of which sounds far easier than it is in reality.

In the early 19th century, moving and transplanting a mature tree was an arduous and protracted task that could take up to two years to fully complete, and it involved transporting the tree horizontally, which often damaged its branches. Barron, as a means of pleasing his boss, the Earl of Harrington at Elvaston Castle in Derbyshire, devised a much quicker way of doing this in order to create gardens full of mature trees. His process of digging trenches around and under the tree's root ball, winching the tree out of position and transporting it vertically, reduced transplanting time to three months. He described his methods in his book *The British Winter Garden: A Practical Treatise on Evergreens* (1852) and in other works. It soon drew the attention of the press and that of Queen Victoria, who asked him to plant a mature silver fir at Osborne House on the Isle of Wight. Barron famously moved a 43ft-high cedar in 1871, as well as the then 800-year-old Buckland yew in Dover in 1880. From the 1830s he became the country's leading expert of this process, as well as a hugely influential conifer expert and nurseryman.

Kew first bought a tree-transplanting machine in 1866 and is known to have had and used several of varying sizes to move trees around the site. One – most probably this large version – was known by the gardeners as 'the Devil' due to the injuries it caused. In 1908, Kew used the 'Barrons' (as it is affectionately known today) to move 16 mature trees including beeches, elms, oaks, ash, ginkgo, *Robinia* and *Carya* to restore Pagoda Vista. At the turn of the millennium, Kew's Barron tree transplanter was completely restored and used again to plant several Atlantic cedars along the Broad Walk, restoring the avenue to its original aesthetic. One side of the Walk was planted using the Barrons, the other with modern machinery.

Today, on a fine late winter's day, the transplanter is seeing the light of day again. Tom, Kevin, Rich and Jamie open the huge noisy roller shutter door of the dedicated storage unit where it is kept in the Stable Yard to give the Barrons its annual inspection and clean. As sunlight floods the room, they look for any changes in its condition, are alert to any evidence of woodworm, and clean away the cobwebs that optimistic spiders have created. The machine is enormous; the oak beams stand above head height and the thick sturdy wheels are chest-high. 'It's a beast,' says Kevin, who has an appreciation for the technicalities of using this machine. 'They must have been so strong to use this – just trying to lift these beams on your shoulders and put them back into place is ridiculous. They are so heavy.' Indeed, even the metal lever for the top windlass is incredibly heavy to pick up, let alone use. Once the cleaning has been done and checks complete, the team are happy that this fascinating piece of equipment is in tip-top condition.

Back in the workshop, Tom pulls out several large colour prints of the Barrons in use during the year 2000, showing the gardeners in Victorian dress planting one of the Atlantic cedars. He also finds and shares a series of photographs taken by E J Wallis around 1900 showing in sequence how a tree was lifted, moved and planted using the machine at Kew. Tom is sure that these record a particular tree on Pagoda Vista. From the position of a deodar and a characterful stone pine in the background (both of which still exist) he deduces that it was a tree planted where a large sweet chestnut now stands on that Vista. The Gang then debate whether the tree shown in its winter form in the photo is, in fact, a sweet chestnut. The living tree looks big enough to have been planted 125 years ago but they're still unsure. It's a tantalizing piece of photographic evidence for Kew's landscape history but more research is required. For now, the Barrons stands ready to play its part in another year of Kew's story when required.

As ever in the Gardens, the process of planting and removal is in perpetual motion. With spring on the horizon, and a spell of fine weather under way, it's time for the Tree Gang to cut down the black pine that they had observed Justin and Isabel scan using LiDAR late last year. By now, Justin, Isabel and colleagues have calculated the carbon content of the pine from the LiDAR scan and have also obtained three equivalent figures derived by using allometric equations to calculate black pine carbon content. Now all they need to do is work out exactly how much carbon is locked up in the scanned pine, which they'll do by cutting down and weighing it, and comparing this result to those from the digital scan and allometric equations.

In order for them to obtain as accurate a figure as possible, they need the Tree Gang to separate out material into sized-based fractions as the tree is slowly razed. This is because wood density varies according to the age of the timber and its position in the tree, and correct density figures will be needed to calculate the tree's above-ground carbon content. This will make for labour-intensive work, so, aside from Arthur, who has taken the week off, all the arborists are present. Even Rich is back for a 'staying-in-touch' day – only the second time he has returned to the Gardens since going on parental leave in November to look after his three-and-a-half-year-old son and one-year-old daughter. 'It turns out you don't get much time to do anything else when you're looking after children,' he jokes.

The Gang make their way to the pine in two tractors and the Kubota buggy. One tractor hauls the wood chipper, the second tractor pulls a trailer, and the buggy tows the arborists' essential black box of kit. They have already weighed the tractors, wood chipper and trailer back at the workshop to ascertain the vehicles' empty weights. Later, once full, they will be weighed again, and the weight of each separate fraction of timber calculated. Parking up on the frosted grass beside the tree, the five unload their equipment and prepare for the task ahead. They assess the form of the tree to decide how best to categorize and separate the material. The pine has a single trunk that Rich measures to be 80cm in diameter at chest level, and which stays a consistent width for much of its 18-metre height. At the top, it splits into four thick, near-vertical stems that each give rise to secondary branches supporting the canopy. There are also a few smaller branches extending from the trunk lower down. Based on the tree's form, the Tree Gang decide to separate the material into six fractions: foliage and stems up to 2cm in diameter; small branches of secondary wood between 2cm and 15cm in diameter; primary timber from 15cm down to the four main forks from the trunk; and the trunk itself in six 3-metre sections.

Today, Tom is to climb the tree and do the cutting, while the others help to winch the removed limbs to the ground and process the wood. They'll take samples from each fraction so Justin and Isabel can measure the wood density of each. While Tom sets up his climbing and rigging lines and heads up into the tree, the others take a guess at what the pine will weigh. Rich had initially guessed 8,000kg before seeing the tree. Now, after considering the tree's height and checking the specific gravity of the species online, he decides to stick with this figure. Will and Cecily discuss what portion of the trunk might equate to a tonne of water, after which Will decides on 5,000kg and Cecily plumps for 11,000kg. And Jamie plucks the figure of 7,500kg from the air. Kevin also has skin in the game having already guessed 10,000kg. They won't find out who's won until the hard work of today – and probably tomorrow as well – is over.

While Tom readies himself in the branches, the ground team start using secateurs and long-handled loppers to remove needles and small branches hanging close to the ground, piling them up in a small mound beside the wood chipper. Then, once all the low-hanging branches have gone, Tom sets to work on high. He attaches a medium-sized branch to the rigging line, calls over the state-of-the-art intercom headphones (a recent addition to the team's kit) that he's 'immediately ready when you are', awaits confirmation that everyone's set, then slices through the branch. Will uses the rope around the winch to slowly lower it until Cecily is able to reach it and haul it across to the processing area. After removing the rope, she cuts the timber into sections. More branches quickly follow suit, with the team dragging the timber to near the chipper, then cutting it up and allocating it to different wood piles. The largest sections of branches are shouldered to the trailer, with the medium-sized sections placed on one mound on the grass and the small twigs and foliage on another. Every so often someone rakes up the smallest pieces of foliage, adding them to the pile, carefully leaving sawdust to be included with the timber. When the stack of branches awaiting processing gets too large, Tom pauses cutting so that the team can catch up. Bent over the wood, snipping rhythmically with their orange loppers, they resemble insects making light work of a leafy feast.

At midday, Cecily reverses the tractor and trailer close to the tree. With much of the canopy now removed, Tom is about to tackle the larger branches. As these will be pretty heavy, the aim is for him to cut one section of large branch off at a time and for the team to use the winch to direct the timber straight into the trailer. The plan works well and the trailer is soon full – and therefore ready for weighing. Back at the workshop, while Cecily carefully manoeuvres the tractor and loaded trailer into position, Tom and Rich lay out two yellow half-metre-square weighing pads just ahead of the front wheels. These are wired to a portable box that has both a screen to display the weight and a mini printer to output a hard copy. Once the scales are in position, Cecily drives the front wheels of the tractor onto the scales, then the rear wheels, and finally the trailer wheels. The weight of each is recorded and added together – this load weighs 1,092kg – then, once the trailer has been emptied, the process is repeated for the empty vehicle. Over the course of the next day and a half, the Gang repeat this process until the tree is reduced to a ground-level stump and all the wood is weighed. The final figure is 10,051kg. Not only does this make Kevin the 'annoyingly accurate' (says Tom) winner of the 'guess the weight competition', but it also means that Justin and Isabel can now calculate how much carbon the tree's timber contains.

The results from scanning the tree yielded a total volume of 8,920 litres – equivalent to almost nine builders' bags of the kind used to deliver bulky materials such as gravel. Multiplying this figure by a wood density estimate for a black pine of 0.417 provided a figure for the dry biomass weight of 3,720kg. Then, with carbon content known to be approximately half of the biomass, multiplying 3,720 by 0.508 gave 1,890kg carbon. By comparison, three separate methodologies of calculating the carbon content using allometric equations yielded widely varying figures. The first, based on diameter at breast height

(DBH), height of tree and location calculated the carbon content to be 1,630kg. The second, employing just DBH and height, arrived at a figure of 1,336kg. And the third, using just DBH, yielded a result of 705kg.

With the weight of the 'wet' tree now known, Justin and Isabel need to freeze-dry the wood samples to remove the water, which will tell them the amount of biomass for each separate fraction of the tree. Tree biomass is essentially carbon plus hydrogen in a biological form, so they will also need to remove the hydrogen part to work out the carbon content for each fraction. Adding up the various results will enlighten them as to how much carbon is actually contained in the whole pine.

'We're using this tree as an experimental tree to develop the methodology, as pines are relatively simple trees,' says Justin. 'The allometric equations are generally underestimating how much carbon is in the trees. We're hoping to show that there's more carbon in the actual tree than suggested from the equations, and that the LiDAR image is giving us a good result – which, for this pine tree, it should do for sure. What we really want to do is then apply this approach to more problematic trees, such as oaks and other species that grow in much more varied forms than pine.' In time, these results will be added to those from similar experiments at Wakehurst that are focused on carbon storage and identifying 'nature-based' approaches to adapting to climate change.

Work is under way to create a new Carbon Garden at Kew, which will highlight the organization's scientific work on nature-based solutions, as well as educating visitors on the role of carbon in keeping Earth functioning, today and in the future. The Garden will be built to the north of the Princess of Wales Conservatory, in an area currently occupied by the Secluded Garden. This area is ripe for renovation, as the Garden was developed more than 30 years ago and has become somewhat dilapidated. The new garden will be arranged into four zones, with exhibits and interpretation that explain: the carbon cycle; why carbon added to the atmosphere by human activities is causing the global climate to change; how approaches and technologies that borrow from nature can help to mitigate climate change; and ways in which humanity will be able to draw on the wealth of the plants on Earth to adapt to climate change. Plantings of shade-loving species, a dry garden and a flower meadow will help to underline the messages portrayed through the Carbon Garden.

The garden is to be constructed near the ancient maidenhair tree (*Ginkgo biloba*), so Tom wants to undertake a survey of it now to ensure that its health is properly monitored and protected. This will also give him the chance to see what maintenance works might be needed and how soon he needs to schedule those to ensure they're completed before the Carbon Garden opens. As Jamie had explained to his autumn tour group in the pouring rain, the ginkgo was one of the first Chinese trees to be planted in Princess Augusta's new small royal botanical garden, having been bought from the specialist London nursery of James Gordon. Gordon was celebrated in his day as a knowledgeable plantsman, nursery owner and seed merchant, or, as Peter Collinson described him 'a most Knowing and Ingenous Man'. Gordon was one of a new breed of nurserymen in England who specialized in bringing 'exotic' species to Britain and he particularly excelled in propagating rare and difficult species. This is exemplified by his having been the first person to import and cultivate not only the ginkgo, but also the Japanese pagoda tree and the Caucasian elm, among others.

At the time that Gordon was first carefully nurturing the ginkgo in Britain, it did not even have a Latin name. It was only when Gordon sent a sample to the Swedish naturalist

Carl Linnaeus that it was named *Ginkgo kaempferi* in 1769, the species name recognizing the German naturalist Engelbert Kaempfer who had first described the tree for Western science in the 17th century. Kew's prize specimen was one of Gordon's first batch of saplings and the first to be planted out in a garden in the UK. Now one of Kew's Old Lions, this tree embodies much of the history of horticulture, the plant trade and the early garden at Kew, and is therefore a living cultural treasure to be nurtured through its maturity.

Ginkgos are now endangered in the mountain forests of China and are most often found planted around temples and in urban areas across China, Japan and Korea. This is a sad state of affairs for one of the world's oldest tree species, which dates back millions of years to the Jurassic period, when dinosaurs roamed the Earth. Individual trees can sometimes live for thousands of years – one in China is thought to be over 3,000 years old, so Kew's tree is potentially still in its infancy. In China, ginkgos are symbols of resilience and healing, and are used in many traditional medicines. The species is dioecious, meaning that there are separate male and female trees. Kew's tree is a male, but it once had a female branch grafted to its side as an experiment. Planters of female trees should be forewarned that in autumn their fruits are extremely smelly, their scent reminiscent of a damp sports kit that has been left in a locker for too long. Despite this olfactory assault, ginkgos of any description, with their delicate lobed, fan-shaped leaves, make elegant and robust additions to gardens and streetscapes.

Tom reaches the ginkgo at first light, well before the Gardens are fully open, so he can easily move around the tree and assess it without disrupting – or attracting the attention of – visitors. He arrives with the usual tools of his tree-inspection trade, including his tablet with the Tree Smart software loaded up, and a metal probe for checking the density of the timber. As he approaches the tree, he looks at the form and health of its canopy, to note, for example, whether it is 'retrenching' (where the outer stems are losing vitality). Then, once he gets to the tree, he starts his systematic inspection from the base up. He searches around the bottom of the trunk, moving leaves and debris to see where the trunk meets the soil, and potentially exposing any fungi. He looks for any abnormal taper at the base of the trunk that might have been caused by over-mulching of the ground, and he pokes inside all the cavities to see if there is any soft bark or rot. This species is unusual in that it grows in obvious 'functional units', where vertical sections of the tree – large 'ropes' of growth – stretch up the trunk and link up to individual branches. Looking at these, it is easy to see which sections are in active growth, as, within these distinct units the bark has pale 'stretch marks' indicating its outward expansion. As he goes about the task, Tom records all his observations on the Tree Smart software.

As Jamie had pointed out on his tour, this individual is full of evidence of old arboricultural works, including where branches have been removed and painted with black Arbrex paint. Such attention is not necessarily historic however, and may have been done as late as the 1970s or 1980s. Tom checks all the wounds and cavities. He points out the acute V-shaped union between this tree's two large trunks (which some people suggest is where two trees fused together from a young age). This kind of branch junction, known as an 'included union', is not ideal in a large tree as it means that the wood is pushing against the opposing limb as it grows. Normally a tree will produce a U-shape between such trunks or limbs. The tree has several tight unions like this, which has led arborists in the past to place bracing in the tree higher up to add structural stability to its several slim trunks. Tight branch unions are quite typical in ginkgos however, so Tom knows this is part of its natural form.

He steps back to consider the canopy to see if there are

any gaps – another indicator of where weak unions between branches exist, and where branches are starting to pull apart. For this he can also consult previous tree inspections to see if any change has become apparent. He is delighted that after several recent storms no material has come off the tree, no movement has occurred, and it is still looking healthy. As part of the inspection Tom needs to record the state of the bracing that already exists in the higher canopy. Bracing needs to be inspected yearly and replaced on a regular schedule. This dynamic system of bracing is a flexible kind known as Cobra bracing, and is made of braided polyester with a 'spreader section' in the middle to aid the natural movement of the branches while restricting how far they can move. Tom describes the middle section of the bracing as working 'a bit like a Chinese finger trap', which, as it stretches, only becomes tighter. This dynamic flexible system of bracing (as opposed to restrictive steel cable bracing) had been seen as the best type to use in this tree in the past.

Tom confirms that they will have to re-brace the tree, but only because it has historically had bracing so they will need to continue to support it in this way. In less famous trees, they tend to significantly reduce the canopy and take weight off the branches rather than install new bracing. In fact, Tom says, these days they remove more bracing than they install. The thinking around how trees put on new wood to support themselves in reaction to the wind and other environmental conditions has changed in recent years. Thinking has also changed on removing crossing branches. Through the work of Dr Duncan Slater, who was among Kevin's tutors at Myerscough College, it is now thought that trees are doing this deliberately to form new branch attachments (where two branches fuse together to form a union) as a kind of natural bracing to aid stability of the canopy. Tom decides that he will have to get up into the tree to inspect the higher branches, and he especially wants to look closely at the woodpecker holes in the one tall straight trunk.

Because this tree is one of the highlights of Kew, and next to a busy path, any changes to it need careful consideration, and safety is a huge part of its management. Taking off branches may alter the outline of the canopy but Tom is keen to point out that if they do a good job of thinning and reducing it visitors will not notice any significant difference. Ginkgos react well to pruning, so he hopes that by making judicious cuts to the longer branches and reducing its size slightly, this tree will put on new healthy growth inside the main canopy. He decides that work on this iconic tree is a high priority. Not only does he want to inspect the upper canopy and nesting holes up close, he also wants to reduce the weight of the outer branches on the tree's long limbs. Doing the work in winter without a full canopy of leaves will also be easier for the team, enabling them to see the whole structure and shape of the tree.

Tom is a man of his word, and by the following week he has acquired a bright green 'Nifty Lift' – a mobile elevated work platform (or MEWP) that can be extended and moved like a crane arm – and gathers the whole team for a day of pruning the outer canopy. Doing this reduction work will allow easier access for climbing at a later date to check and then replace the bracing. The Tree Gang members arrive one by one in convoy – Jamie by bike, Arthur driving the Kubota, Will in a tractor pulling a large blue trailer, and Tom and Cecily with the MEWP. It's a mild winter's morning, with grey clouds scudding across a pale blue sky, and the early pre-dawn rain has, thankfully, stopped. Arthur sets up the temporary green fencing and Tree Cutting warning signs to protect the public, while Will steers the tractor and trailer into position ready to take the wood pruned from the tree. Tom drives the MEWP under the canopy of the ginkgo and judges where to park it so they can begin to access the outer branches. The manoeuvrable arm and platform on this Nifty Lift can reach 17 metres high so it should enable Tom to get to all but the uppermost stems and reach the outer canopy, which would be harder to do through climbing alone.

Tom climbs onto the platform and attaches his safety harness to it. Although, in theory, the platform can take two people, only Tom is using it today as he is taking up a chainsaw which needs to be operated at a safe distance from others. He is also taking up a variety of hand tools. It is extremely unusual for an arborist to approach a tree with secateurs, but this is exactly what Tom starts with. He carefully assesses which of the smaller branches within the mop of outer stems can be taken away to help reduce the weight on each branch without affecting the look of the canopy. He deftly snips and saws away at a variety of lateral and apical stems. This act of lightly reducing the canopy will create a healthier, more stable crown and place less stress on the tree. Controlling and moving the MEWP arm from up in the platform to manoeuvre around the outer canopy is slow methodical work. Getting to just the right place takes patience, and although Tom is quick to make decisions about where he wants to prune, this is slow work by necessity. The benefit, however, is the great view over the Gardens from this elevation, taking in everything from the Orangery and the Broad Walk to the wider view over the Gardens beyond the Palm House.

On the ground, the team are communicating with Tom about where to head next and which branches they think could go. It is only when he gets to the top of the ginkgo that Tom can see that previous arborists have topped its branches before and reduced its height. Where such work has taken place, Tom must thin out the bushier growth resulting from old pruning cuts. He takes out any larger branches with a small chainsaw using step-cuts to slowly take the weight off the branch until he gets to the final pruning cut. Hopefully, from this point the tree will grow back in a more natural way. Tom throws down manageable chunks of branches to the team below, who carefully step forward at intervals in their protective gear to load these into the trailer, where Jamie is crunching them down underfoot to create more space.

Before long the first trailer is full, and after an hour and a half they need a break and to step back to see how the one side of the tree they have completed looks. At this point they can judge the tree from different angles and see if Tom needs to go back to adjust any cuts. It's a slightly tense moment – have they done a good enough job? After suitable refreshments and a fresh look at the tree, they continue the work, and by mid-afternoon they have finished the whole canopy. Remarkably, it is only clear by comparing before and after photos that work has been done. To the visitors who are now strolling by on the freshly swept path below, this iconic tree is as beautiful as it has always been, and it will also now be less vulnerable to winter storms.

British winters are notoriously temperamental, but when Storm Éowyn barrels across the country in late January its force comes as a surprise to many. Probably the strongest storm of the past decade, it cuts power to a million homes, and blocks roads and railways. Northern Ireland and Scotland are particularly hard hit, with gusts reaching 183 and 145 kilometres (114 and 90 miles) per hour respectively in the two countries. All four of the gardens managed by Royal Botanic Garden Edinburgh (RBGE) – Edinburgh, Dawyck, Logan and Benmore – are badly hit, with more than 400 trees felled across them and many others damaged. The Edinburgh site alone loses 15 significant trees, with 26 more damaged. The garden's tallest specimen, a deodar cedar (*Cedrus deodara*), is snapped in two, while a yellow buckeye (*Aesculus flava*) blows apart, taking off the lower five branches of a nearby rare

Himalayan hazel (*Corylus jacquemontii*). Deputy Curator Will Hinchliffe estimates that at this site alone it will take a month to clear the fallen trees and branches, and an entire year to complete the remedial pruning work to the damaged trees.

In need of assistance, RBGE reaches out to the Tree Gang and the decision is taken that Tom, Cecily, Jamie and Arthur will spend a week helping at the gardens. A van is duly hired and loaded up with kit, and the team make the long drive to Dawyck Botanical Garden, a 26-hectare (65-acre) site in Stobo village, near Peebles, 48 kilometres (30 miles) or so south of Edinburgh. In the hills of the Scottish Borders, the Garden is renowned for its arboretum, which includes some of Britain's most significant trees. Dawyck's oldest specimen is a silver fir (*Abies alba*) dating back to 1680, and the tallest are the Garden's many giant redwoods (*Sequoiadendron giganteum*), which all stand in excess of 50 metres tall.

For Cecily, visiting Dawyck is particularly special; not only is it close to her childhood home, where her parents still live, but she is reunited with Will Hinchliffe, along with RBGE arborist Peter Wilson, who she had first met when she was studying for her Diploma in Horticulture with Plantsmanship at RBGE in 2017. 'When I was on my arb placement as a student, when we helped to dismantle the massive sweet chestnut tree at

Edinburgh that was in decline, Peter was up in the cherry picker doing the cutting,' she explains. 'They were both a large part of my journey into arb. They were really encouraging of my work experience at Kew in 2018 during the holidays when I was still a student in Edinburgh – it was the connection between Edinburgh and Kew that made it possible. And now we've come to help the teams at Dawyck and Benmore, and they are still on the tools after all these years.'

The next day, with the weather cold and snowing, the Gang set to work to help restore some order to the arboretum. Ahead of their arrival, the Gardens' staff have marked trees in need of attention, so the Tree Gang split into two teams, each with one person climbing the tree and the other one supporting on the ground. Most of the trees they work on are Douglas firs (*Pseudotsuga menziesii*), a good number of which were grown from seed collected by Scottish botanist David Douglas himself, after whom they are named. Douglas made several expeditions to North America in the early 19th century, introducing the Douglas fir into cultivation in 1827. He also introduced several other conifers to the UK including the noble fir (*Abies procera*) and Sitka spruce (*Picea sitchensis*). The Gang spend three days here working on these magnificent heritage trees.

'They were really big trees, absolutely massive,' says Tom later. 'It's really cool climbing Douglas firs and these are original David Douglas introductions planted in the early 1820s and 1830s. It was still snowing when I went up one of them; it was a really big tree and when I got [to the top] the view was incredible, right across the gardens and the valley. It was quite a unique climb, and a little bit of a career highlight. We got the work that we hoped to get done on all the trees apart from one.' Arthur also enjoyed the opportunity to get some climbing in. 'I climbed three or four Douglas firs,' he says. 'Some of them were complete monsters; our ropes weren't long enough [to get all the way up], so I only went up halfway on most of them. I was taking out some of the hanging limbs [from the storm]. It was a great opportunity, and great fun to meet the other guys as well.'

From Dawyck the team travel to Benmore Botanic Garden, which lies in a mountainside setting north of Dunoon on the Cowal Peninsula. Much larger than Dawyck, at 48.5 hectares (120 acres), the damage here is more extensive, with over 300 trees lost. The Gang drive around with the Garden's staff, surveying the devastation and helping to identify dangerous 'hangers' for removal. As well as having razed entire rows of mature trees, the storm has left smaller trees lying over paths, presenting a hazard to visitors. The team spend the rest of the day clearing what they can.

The next day, the weather takes another turn for the worse, with winds of 97 kilometres (60 miles) an hour sweeping in, so no climbing can take place on their final day. Benmore has a problem with *Phytophthora ramorum*, a fungal-like organism that kills a wide range of trees and shrubs, particularly larch, so the Gang take time to thoroughly clean their kit, ready to hang up to dry in the workshop 'like spaghetti' on their return. 'The damage caused by Storm Éowyn is a stark reminder of the increasing frequency and intensity of extreme weather events due to climate change,' comments Kevin, back at Kew.

Lately, Kevin's work to prepare for the climate shifts to come has been gaining him accolades, and awareness of his research on sourcing resilient trees for the future climate is spreading. Just before Christmas, in front of staff, students and volunteers at the last regular All Staff Talk of the year, Director Richard Deverell had highlighted the challenges facing the living collections due to climate change. But he'd also hailed the success of the Landscape Succession Plan, and the addition of new climate resilient species (including the rare *Quercus pontica* from Georgia) to the Arboretum that year. In the spirit of celebrating the year, three prestigious 'William Aiton medals' had been awarded at the end of Richard's talk. The coveted bronze-coloured medals, each sculpted with a relief of the Palm House on the front, are named after Kew's very first curator of the botanic gardens in the 18th century and are only given to those who have contributed significantly to the work and mission of Kew.

Richard had awarded the medal for 'horticultural achievement' to Kevin, telling his assembled peers that 'Kevin's work on the Landscape Succession Plan will have a lasting legacy, providing managers of important scientific and amenity tree collections with a tool to help inform the selection process. His work is widely regarded as leading in this field ... further enhancing our reputation.' He went on to applaud Kevin for his dedication and enthusiasm as a 'brilliant communicator and advocate for Kew'. Coming at the end of what had been an extremely busy year for Kevin, this recognition in front of all Kew staff was an important celebration of his research and the many forms of outreach he had done regarding its implications. Today, however, it means that he's more in demand than ever, with people both at Kew and beyond wanting to hear about his research and the Landscape Succession Plan – and the implications of climate change on trees, particularly in urban settings.

Late winter sees Kevin talking at two meetings hosted by Kew. The first is a networking meeting for the London Urban Forest Partnership, a group of organizations collaborating to protect, manage and enhance the capital's trees and woodlands. Eighty people attend, including the Deputy Mayor of London and representatives from organizations including Forest Research, the Woodland Trust, The Conservation Volunteers, Trees for Cities and The Orchard Project. The themes of presentations range from how to improve the equity and capacity of London's tree initiatives and workforce to managing urban deer. The Greater London Authority (GLA) has recently asked Kevin to apply his model to look at the vulnerability of London's urban tree canopy under climate change, work that will contribute to the Urban Tree Strategy for Greater London. At the meeting, Kevin outlines the work he is doing for the GLA – which includes using modelling and trait data to rank the suitability of particular tree species to London's future climate – and then takes questions.

'I gave a 20-minute presentation followed by a 20-minute question-and-answer session, which felt like it was going on forever,' he admits. 'I'd answer one question and five more hands would go up. We had an interesting discussion, though. We talked about using native species versus non-natives; the Community Orchard Group asked about resilience in apples; and we also talked about subsidence. A lot of tree officers are obsessed with subsidence, so I said to them, "this work will help you, because you don't want to plant a high-water-demanding tree in areas where you've got high subsidence claims, so if you use this work and look at low-water-demanding trees such as *Tilia tomentosa* and *Tilia dasystyla* then you're not going to have that issue as much". And we talked about cultural change, about people having to accept that we're going to need to give up "grey spaces" – in other words parking spaces and pavements – in order to build in green infrastructure to create the cooling that we need.'

Four days after the meeting, Kevin is back on stage again, at a meeting entitled 'Planting the urban future landscape'. This time, he gives a joint presentation with Simon Toomer and Tom Freeth on Kew's Landscape Succession Plan, to an audience encompassing policymakers from local authorities, nursery specialists and non-governmental organizations. After the talk, industry professionals field questions from the audience. This panel includes Phillip Hall, Nursery Manager from Hillier Nurseries, Dr Andrew Hirons of Myerscough

College, and Anne Jaluzot, London Urban Forest Plan Coordinator, as well as representatives from the Department for Environment, Food and Rural Affairs. 'What was great was having the nurseries talking about the issues we're going to have to select new species and get them into trade,' says Kevin. 'The biggest problem is going to be getting these trees into trade, because you've got to build the stock levels up. And using clones is not ideal from the point of genetic diversity. Phil [Hall] was saying that people have got to get used to not having the perfect tree all the time; landscape architects use all these lollipops. It's again about how we manage that cultural shift.'

While it's great for Kevin that his research is gaining respect, a slight issue is that he still needs to actually finish his own studies. Having had confirmation that his research can contribute to both a master's and a PhD, Kevin is currently writing up his master's thesis on the modelling aspect of his research. Once this is done, he will turn his attention to his PhD, which he is undertaking 'by publication'. This means that he has to submit four corresponding papers (for peer-reviewed publication) in order to be awarded the doctoral degree. The first paper will be on using modelling as a screening tool to identify where to source trees for the future climate. The second will consider the link between the modelling outputs and plant traits, such as turgor loss point and wood density. The third will be on how to use the trait data to refine the modelling further, 'which no one has ever done before,' says Kevin. And the fourth will be a critical analysis of the research undertaken. He's hoping to complete the PhD within three years.

In the meantime, he's not resting on his laurels. Keen to see the concept of urban tree resilience incorporated into Kew's Science Strategy, Kevin has spent the morning presenting his research findings to Alexandre Antonelli, Kew's Director of Science, and all the leaders of scientific strands at the Gardens. As an arborist, he is the first horticulturalist to present to this team of eminent scientists, an experience he describes as 'probably the most nerve-racking thing I've ever done, like being on *Dragon's Den*.' Ultimately, he's hoping to develop a joint project uniting science and horticulture at Kew – such as on urban pollination – in order to generate new data that can also be fed back into his climate model.

Just as the second half of the 19th century was a seminal period for Kew's Arboretum, during which William and Joseph Hooker planted thousands of trees in designed family groups, and William Bean and William Dallimore started to become the country's foremost tree experts, so the work of today's Tree Gang will very likely be looked back on as a key moment in Kew's history. As the first team to face the real impacts of climate change on the Gardens, they have approached the challenge in the best way they know how: by drawing on the history and science physically embodied in the Arboretum and combining it with their arboricultural knowledge and expertise to ensure its survival in the future. After a long period in which the balance of science and pleasure in the Arboretum have tipped back and forth, the scientific value of this remarkable collection is being recognized once more – just as its pioneering creators intended.

'This is why places like Kew are so important,' enthuses Kevin. 'We have always done plant collecting so we have trees from around the world in one place. We represent plants from around the globe in different ecosystems in one place, and although that's a small study set it can allow you to identify trends and highlight new areas to focus on. And what makes Kew unique is that we have research facilities. I go to arboreta around the world but no one else has a Jodrell Laboratory; the work I'm doing now would be impossible anywhere else in the world. To have the ability to go and look at scanning electron microscopes and study vessels that are atom-sized is incredible. The research we can do here is at the forefront of biodiversity and climate-change studies, and that's what my research has proved.'

Only time will tell whether using seeds from trees that have evolved to tolerate dry and hot conditions will help to future-proof Europe's botanic gardens and cities from the human-forced global climatic shift that is under way. However, the Romanian and Georgian seedlings growing in the Arboretum Nursery offer hope that they will, and that the specimens destined to replace the likes of this year's fallen beech, eucalyptus and black pine will fare better. Outside in the Gardens, the continuing good health of the *Quercus castaneifolia* and other steppe and Mediterranean plants is also a positive sign. For now, though, the Tree Gang have more immediate concerns. Sap is starting to rise, the cycle of life is continuing, and spring is around the corner. With it will come trees to climb, branches to prune, moths on the move and events to support – not least a festival-length homage to trees showcasing Kew's first-ever outdoor digital artwork commission. This momentous year in the life of Kew's Tree Gang is drawing to a close but, for Kevin, Tom, Will, Jamie, Cecily, Rich, Arthur and Sal, a new one is about to unfurl.

Selected Reading

Alcorn, Keith, ' "His utter unfitness for a commercial collector": Sponsorship of exotic plant collecting in early nineteenth-century Britain', *Journal of the History of Collections*, 35(2) (July 2023), pp. 347–62; https://doi.org/10.1093/jhc/fhac032

Bean, W J, *Trees and Shrubs Hardy in the British Isles Vol 1–4*, 8th edition (John Murray, 1989).

Bean, W J, and William Thistleton-Dyer, *The Royal Botanic Gardens, Kew: Historical and Descriptive* (Cassell and Company, 1908).

Besant, J W, 'Plantae Henryanae', *The Gardeners' Chronicle*, vol. 98 (9 November 1935), pp. 334–35.

Cloake, John, *Palaces and Parks of Richmond and Kew: Vol. 2: Richmond Lodge and the Kew Palaces*, limited edition (Phillimore & Co. Ltd, 1996).

Davison, Fiona, *The Hidden Horticulturists: The Untold Story of the Men Who Shaped Britain's Gardens* (Atlantic Books, 2019).

Davison, Fiona, *An Almost Impossible Thing: The Radical Lives of Britain's Pioneering Women Gardeners* (Little Toller Books, 2024).

Del Tredici, Peter, 'Natural regeneration of *Ginkgo biloba* from downward growing cotyledonary buds (basal chichi)', American Journal of Botany, 79 (5) (May 1992), pp.522-530; https://doi.org/10.1002/j.1537-2197.1992.tb14588.x

Desmond, Ray, *The History of Kew*, 2nd revised edition (Royal Botanic Gardens, 2007).

Drayton, Richard, *Nature's Government: Science, Imperial Britain and the 'Improvement' of the World* (Yale University Press, 2000).

Fry, Carolyn, *Trees: 10 Things You Should Know* (Seven Dials, 2023).

Harrison, Christina, *Kew's Big Trees*, new edition (Kew Publishing, 2025).

Harrison, Christina, and Tony Kirkham, *Remarkable Trees*, 2nd edition (Thames and Hudson Ltd, 2024).

Harrison, Christina, Dan Luscombe and Simon Toomer, *Bedgebury Pinetum* (Kew Publishing, 2025).

Harrison, Christina, and Martyn Rix, *Treasured Trees*, new edition (Kew Publishing, 2024).

Hobhouse, Penelope, *The Story of Gardening: A Cultural History of Famous Gardens from around the World* (Pavilion Books, 2019).

Hourigan, Christina, 'A global arboretum: The case of the Royal Botanic Gardens, Kew', (Royal Holloway, University of London and Royal Botanic Gardens, Kew, PhD thesis, forthcoming 2026).

IPCC, 2021: *Climate Change 2021: The Physical Science Basis. Contribution of Working Group I to the Sixth Assessment Report of the Intergovernmental Panel on Climate Change* [Masson-Delmotte, V, P Zhai, A Pirani, S L Connors, C Péan, S Berger, N Caud, Y Chen, L Goldfarb, M I Gomis, M Huang, K Leitzell, E Lonnoy, J B R Matthews, T K Maycock, T Waterfield, O Yelekçi, R Yu and B Zhou (eds)], (Cambridge University Press, 2023); doi:10.1017/9781009157896

Johnston, Mark, *The Tree Experts: A History of Professional Arboriculture* (Windgather Press, 2021).

Keogh, Luke, *The Wardian Case: How a Simple Box Moved Plants and Changed the World* (University of Chicago Press, 2020).

Koch, Hauke, and Philip C Stevenson, 'Do linden trees kill bees? Reviewing the causes of bee deaths on silver linden (*Tilia tomentosa*)', *Biology Letters*, 13(9) (September 2017); https://doi.org/10.1098/rsbl.2017.0484

Kühn, Nicola, et al, 'Globally important plant functional traits for coping with climate change', *Frontiers of Biogeography*, 13(4) (2021); doi:10.21425/F5FBG53774

Liddle, Tamsin, and Peter Robinson, *William Barron: The Victorian Landscape Gardener* (Amberley Publishing, 2022).

Loudon, J C, *Arboretum et Fruticetum Britannicum, or: The Trees and Shrubs of Britain, Native and Foreign, Hardy and Half-Hardy, Pictorially and Botanically Delineated, and Scientifically and Popularly Described* ... (privately printed, 1838); https://www.biodiversitylibrary.org/item/121003

Martinez del Castillo, Edurne, et al, 'Climate-change-driven growth decline of European beech forests', *Communications Biology* 5, article no. 163 (March 2022); https://doi.org/10.1038/s42003-022-03107-3

Nicoll, Alasdair, 'Exploring nature-based solutions to oak processionary moth', *The ARB Magazine* 205 (Summer 2024).

Sjöman, Henrik, and Arit Anderson, *The Essential Tree Selection Guide: For Climate Resilience, Carbon Storage, Species Diversity and Other Ecosystem Benefits* (Filbert Press, 2023).

Sjöman, Henrik, et al, 'Resilient trees for urban environments: The importance of intraspecific variation', *Plants, People, Planet* (July 2024); https://doi.org/10.1002/ppp3.10518

Willis, Kathy, and Carolyn Fry, *Plants: From Roots to Riches*, reprint edition (John Murray, 2014).

Websites

https://www.treesandshrubsonline.org/
https://www.iucnredlist.org/
https://barnescommon.org.uk/conservation/species-management/black-poplar-project/
https://kewguild.org.uk/journal/
For Kew's Landscape Succession Plan, World Heritage Site Management Plan and its State of the World's Plants and Fungi documents, and for the latest Science and Sustainability strategies, go to and search: www.kew.org
Plant names, synonyms and native ranges have been checked on Kew's Plants of the World Online: https://powo.science.kew.org/

Index

Abies 141–2, 206
  A. alba 239
  A. beshnazuensis 113
  A. cephalonica 154
  A. fargesii 90
  A. homolepsis 113
  Kew collection 112–13
  A. nordmanniana 122
  A. procera 240
Acacia 10
Acer 10
  A. campestre 132
  A. cappadocicum 130
  A. heldreichii subsp. *trautvetteri* 141, 172
  A. saccharinum 102
  A. tataricum 169
acorns 57, 94, 119, 171
Action Oak 64
acute oak decline 64
Adamson, Tom 51
adaptation, climate change 69, 75, 7 7–8, 79–84, 85–9, 91–2
Adiantum pedatum 146
Aesculus 3, 10

A. californica 58
A. flava 238
Agrilus planipennis 62
air pollution 207
air-pots 214–15, 216
air spades 35, 41, 149
aircraft crashes 4
Aiton, William 6, 242–3
Alcorn, Keith 7
alders 90, 139
All Staff Talks 242–3
Alnus
  A. gultinosa subsp. *barbata* 139
  A. lusitanica 90
American basswood 88
American pin oaks 54
Anderson, Arit 100
Antonelli, Alexandre 247
apprenticeships 15, 25, 31–2, 106, 144, 185–6, 190–3, 201–2
Araucaria araucana 206
The ARB Magazine 51–3
Arboretum
  arrangement 10–11
  climate change planning 69–71, 89–91, 114, 242, 248–9

Arboretum – *cont'd.*
    purpose 113–14, 136–7, 160
    size 4
    zones 36
arboretum, first use of term 8
Arboretum Records 32–3
Arboricultural Association (AA) 25, 51
arboriculture
    historical techniques 106–9, 110–12, 145, 146–7, 232
    industry employment levels 22–3
    training courses 15, 21–2, 24–5, 27, 38, 39, 73, 74, 105, 185–6, 192–3, 201–2
Arbrex 106, 232
archives 32
Argyll, 3rd Duke of (Archibald Campbell) 6
Armillaria sp. 102
Arnold Arboretum, Boston, USA 210
Aromia bungii 62
artwork commissions 249
ash 10, 61–2, 131
ash dieback 61–2
Asian sawtooth oaks 54
aspens 81
Atlantic cedars 204, 207
atlas cedars 204
Augusta, Princess of Wales 5–6, 81
awards 242–3

Bacillus thuringiensis 45
bacteria, pest treatments 45
Baishan fir 113
Balanites aegyptiaca 121
Balkan maple 141, 172
Banks, Joseph 6–7, 9
Barley, Richard 69
Barron, William 217–19
Barron's tree transplanter 217–21
Bartlett Tree Experts 48, 49, 50–1
Batumi, Georgia 124
bay laurel 121
BBC 98–9
Bean, William Jackson 74–5, 108–9, 206, 207, 208

Bedgebury Pinetum 35, 109, 207–8
beeches
    climate change 12, 89, 94
    common 90
    European 3, 5, 12–13, 41, 89, 94, 122
    oriental 94, 130, 131, 133–4, 140
    southern 10
bees 76–7
Benmore Botanic Garden 241–2
Berkshire College of Agriculture 192
Besant, J W 212–13
Betula pendula subsp. *pendula* 89
BGCI (Botanic Gardens Conservation International) 75, 81
biochar 149
biodiversity
    Kew collection 185
    Natural Area 163, 164–5, 198–9
    oaks 53, 163, 198–9
    understorey 58
biosecurity 60
bioturbation 150
birches 89, 94, 154
bird cherry 131
birds, pest control 52
black alder 139
black locust tree 4
black pines 28, 193–5, 196–8, 221–3
black poplars 164–7
blackthorn 125
bladdernut 170
blue gum 79
Blue Peter 42–4
bluebells 3, 162
Bluebells and Broomsticks festival 48
Botanic Gardens Conservation International (BGCI) 75, 81
box 154
bracing 233, 234–5
branch unions 232–3, 234
brittle cinder fungus 13, 41
Broad Walk 204, 219–20
broadleaf spindle tree 131
Brookes, Ruth 162, 163–7, 202
bubble flower 4

INDEX

buckeyes 3, 238
Buckland yew 219
bumblebees 76–7
Burley, Kay 69
Bute, 3rd Earl (John Stuart) 6

caffeine and bees 76–7
California buckeye 58
cambium savers 18, 20
cambium tissue 59
Camellia japonica 'Kingyo- subaki' 190
Cameraria ohridella 62
Campbell, Archibald, 3rd Duke of Argyll 6
Campbell's magnolia 11
Canary Islands juniper 180
Canine Assisted Pest Eradication 62
canopy lifting 26
Cant, Beckham 167
Capel Manor college, Enfield 27
Cappadocian maple 130
carbon biomass 195, 198, 221–7
Carbon Garden 228–9
Carcelia iliaca 52
Carl Linnaeus 229
Caroline, Queen 5
Carpinus
    C. betulus 90, 131, 169
    C. orientalis 130, 169
Carya 3
Castanea sativa 24–5, 142
Catalpa 10
caterpillars 44–53
Caucasian elm 75, 138–9, 229
Caucasian nettle tree 3
Caucasian oak 142
Caucasian spruce 122
Caucasian whortleberry 141
Caucasus 71, 75, 92, 93, 110, 120–2, 127, 141
cavitation 80–1, 95
Cedar of Lebanon 206
Cedar Vista 9, 207
cedars 154, 157, 204, 205, 207, 219, 238
Cedrus
    C. atlantica 204, 207

C. deodara 238
C. libani 206
cell turgor pressure 80
Celtis
    C. caucasica 3
    C. cerasifera 90
Cephalotaxus 207
Chamaerops humilis 186–7
Champion Trees 55, 71–3, 91
Charlotte, Queen 161
cherries 9, 11, 131
cherry hackberry 90
cherry plum 131
Cherry Walk 11
Chesham Gardens, Manchester 33
chestnut-leaved oak 54, 55–6, 71–5, 91, 93
chi-chis 146
Children's Garden 156, 177–8
Chilean myrtle 187
Chimonanthus praecox 188
Chinese lime 88
Chinquapin oak 96
chlorophyll 119
Chokushi-Mon 14
Christmas at Kew 87, 158, 159–60, 186
Christmas barbecue 198, 203
Church, Rich
    background 21–2
    carbon biomass 222, 223
    parental leave 201, 210, 222
    pea-light tree 158–9
Chusan palm 186–7
clay 149
climate change
    adaptation 69, 75, 77–8, 79–84, 85–9, 91–2
    Arboretum planning 69–71, 89–91, 114, 242, 248–9
    Carbon Garden 228–9
    disease and growing seasons 64
    Paris Agreement 84
    predictions overview 12, 84–5
    rainfall 85
    storms 176–7, 180, 238, 242

climbing equipment 15, 17–19
climbing techniques 19–21, 23–4, 28, 112, 133–4
clones 138
coastal redwood 4, 208
collectors 7, 9
Collinson, Peter 229
common ash 131
common beech 90
common hazel 125
common lime 89–90, 100
common medlar 139
common pear 170
Commonwealth War Graves Commission 144
composting 151–3
cones 204
conifers 9, 10 *see also* firs; pines; Pinetum; spruces
  air pollution 207
  drought adaptation 79, 141
  layered planting 168
  needle blights 62, 194
conservation 125–6, 137, 165, 189, 209–10
Conservation Volunteers 244
Constable, John 164
Cook, Abby 42–4
cork oak 188–9
Cornelian cherry 131, 139
Cornus mas 131
Corsican pine 4
Corylus
  C. avellana 125
  C. jacquemontii 238
cow parsley 3
Crataegus 186
  C. azarolus 139
  C. orientalis 125
Crimean lime 75, 88, 90
cryopreservation 57
Cryptomeria 207
Culture Creative 156
Cunningham, Allan 7
Cupressus sempervirens 91

curry plant 188
Curtis-Machin, Raoul 69
cut test 171–2
cypress oaks 46
cypresses 91, 121, 128, 206

Daily Mail 69
Dallimore, William 32, 35, 109–10, 207, 208
Dalmain, Sal 94
Darwin, Charles 206
Davies-Robertson, Jake 186–7, 188, 193
Davison, Fiona 31
dawn redwoods 208
Dawyck Botanical Garden 239–41
deadwooding 26, 198–203
Del Tredici, Peter 146
Demain, Sal
  background 135
  black poplars 164, 165–6, 167
  Nursery supervision 173–5
  propagation 210
  seed collection 120, 123, 130, 134–5, 170–3
dendrometers 63, 65
deodar cedar 238
deodar cedars 205, 221
Desmond, Ray 161, 206
Deverell, Richard 242–3
Digby, Mathilda 198
Diplodia sapinea 62
disabilities 44
Discovery Days 144–50
disease
  acute oak decline 64
  fungal infections 5, 13, 41, 61–2, 241
  microclimate effects 60–1
  tree assessments 40, 41–2
  UK arrivals 61–3
dogs, fungal disease identification 62
Dothistroma septosporum 62
Douglas, David 240–1
Douglas firs 240
Dow, Chrissie 28

INDEX

downy oak 94
drought 71, 74, 79–80, 91, 94–6, 132, 176, 207
Dutch Elm Disease 62
dwarf fan palm 186–7

Egyptian balsam 121
elms 62, 75, 138–9, 229
emerald ash borer 62
English oak 53, 63, 64, 79, 89, 90, 92, 96–7, 198–9
environmental adaptation 69, 75, 77–8, 79–84, 85–9, 91–2
Escallonia illinita 188
Eucalyptus 10
  E. globulus 79
  E. parvula 177–8
Euonymus latifolious 131
European beech 3, 5, 12–13, 41, 89, 94, 122
European hornbeam 131, 139, 175
European larch 211
evolution 77, 78
Exeter, University of 61
extinction threats 125, 127, 142, 177, 209

Fabaceae 10
Fagaceae *see also Quercus*
  F. orientalis 94, 130, 133
  F. sylvatica 3, 5, 94, 133
  F. x taurica 94, 133–4, 175
Farges fir 90
fastigiate growth 138
Fatsia japonica 187
field maple 131–2
firs 90, 112–13, 122, 126, 154, 206, 239, 240
First World War 29–30, 32–3
flies as pest control method 52
flooding 86
food production 59
Forest Research 12, 62, 208, 244
forestry 34
Forestry Commission 165

Fraxinus 10
  F. ornus 131
Freda, Anna Belle 33
Frederick, Prince of Wales 5
Freeth, Tom 93, 210, 217, 245
fricton devices 20–1
Friends of Barnes Common 165
Fry, Tom
  background 38–9
  Barron's tree transplanter 220–1
  deadwooding 199–200, 202–3
  on historical techniques 106–7
  pea-light tree 158–9
  planning work 35–7
  pruning 235–6
  seed collection 120, 123, 129, 141–2, 143–4
  stump removal 103
  tree assessments 229, 231–4
  tree climbing 133, 240–1
  tree planting 210, 211–12, 214–17
  tree removal 177–8, 223–4, 225
fungal infections 5, 13, 41, 61–2, 102–3, 108, 241
fungi, mycorrhizal 153

The Gardeners' Chronicle 29, 30
genetic diversity of trees 57–8
genotypes 78, 92
geoinjectors 149
George II 5
George III 6, 7
Georgia
  climate and habitats 119–22
  Niko Ketskhoveli Institute of Botany (IoB) 122–3, 125–7
  seed collection 124–6, 129–34, 138–44, 167–8, 170
  Tbilisi 123, 127–9, 137
Georgian snow rose 141
giant redwoods 239
Gilpin, William Sawrey 28
Ginkgo biloba 4, 119, 138, 145–7, 228–38
glasshouses 9

golden oak 57
golden rain tree 90
Gordon, James 6, 138, 145, 229
Gori, Georgia 124
Gothenburg Botanical Garden 99–100, 120, 123, 124, 130, 169
Great British Trees 146
Great Storm of 1987 71, 148
great tits 52
Greater London Authority (GLA) 244
Greek fir 154
Gregg, Arthur
   apprenticeship 185–6, 188, 192–3
   background 191–2
   deadwooding 199, 200, 201–2, 203
   tree climbing 241
   tree planting 210, 211–12, 214–17
growth cycles 58–9
growth shapes 138

Hall, Phillip 245, 246
Hall, Tony 165
Halloween trail 155–7
Hampstead Heath 51–2
Hampton Court Palace 144
Harcourt Aboretum 23, 27–8
Harcourt, Vernon 28
Harding, Will
   background 26–7
   carbon biomass 223
   deadwooding 199
   oak processionary moth (OPM) 47
   pea-light tree 158
   perfumery 211
   tree removal 224
Harrisson, Olive 31
hawthorns 125, 186
The Hay Wain (Constable) 164
hazels 125, 238
Health and Safety Regulations 17–18
   see also safety
Hedera 126
hemlocks 206
Henry, Augustine 212–13
hickories 3

Highgate Wood, London 51–2
Hill, Arthur 207
Hillier Nurseries 210, 245
Himalayan hazel 238
Hinchliffe, Will 238
Hirons, Andrew 245
hollies 3, 10, 130, 186
hollows, identification 41–2
holm oak 90, 91
honey fungus 102–3
Hooker, Joseph 9, 29, 160, 205, 206, 207
Hooker, William 8–9, 56, 205
hop hornbeam 90
hornbeams 90, 106–7, 130, 131, 139, 140, 175
horse chestnut leaf miner 62
horse chestnuts 3, 10, 119
horses, stable manure 151, 152
horticulture, training courses 24–5, 31–2, 135–6
Hortus kewensis 205
hoverflies 3
Hungarian oak 94, 154
Hyde Park Barracks 151
Hymenoscyphus fraxineus 61–2

Iberian alder 90
Ilex 3, 130
Ilia State University 122
Indian bean trees 10
Intergovernmental Panel on Climate Change (IPCC) 84
International Conifer Conservation Programme 210
International Society of Arboriculture (ISA) 39
International Union for the Conservation of Nature (IUCN) 138, 177, 209
IoB (Niko Ketskhoveli Institute of Botany), Ilia State University 122–3, 125–7
Irish yew 206
ironwoods 75

INDEX

irrigation 81–2
Italian cypress 91
ITV Evening News 69
ivy 126

Jaluzot, Anne 245
Japanese allspice 188
Japanese cypress 206
Japanese Douglas-fir 209
Japanese Gateway 14
Japanese pagoda tree 4, 106, 145, 229
Japanese snowbell 58
Jodrell Laboratory 96, 248
Johnston, Mark 34, 112
Jones, Ben 23, 28
Jones, Dean 50
Joshua, Lucy H. 30, 33
Juglans 3
junipers 180, 206
Juniperus cedrus 180

Kaarbon Tech 36
Kaempfer, Engelbert 230
Kerr, William 7
Kew Arboricultural Apprenticeship 15, 25, 106, 185–6, 190–3, 201–2
Kew Diploma in Horticulture 135–6
Kew Gardens
  All Staff Talks 242–3
  becomes public botanic garden 7–8
  biodiversity 185
  foundation 5–6
  Hortus kewensis 205
  purpose 160–1
Kew Guild 110
Kew Guild Journal 30, 33, 34
Kew Mutual Improvement Society 30
Kikodze, David 122, 123, 124, 126–7, 143
Kindt, Roeland 83
King William's Temple 188
Kirkham, Tony 47, 73, 74, 148
Koch, Hauke 76–7
Koelreuteria paniculata 90
Koyama's spruce 209

Kretzschmaria deusta 13
Kybean 177
Kyushu lime 88

Ladies Walk, Hampshire 38
Lancaster University 74
Landscape Succession Plan 89, 137, 167–8, 242, 243, 245
Lanhydrock Park, Cornwall 163
larches 62, 207, 210, 211, 213
large black fly 52
large-leafed lime 88
Larix 207, 211
  L. decidua var. *polonica* 210, 211
Laurus nobilis 121
LBC 69
Le Sueur, Denis 111–12
leachate 152
leaf turgor loss point 80, 95–6, 132
leaves
  autumn changes 119
  drought adaptation 79
  seedlings 175
legume family 10
library 74, 111
LiDAR (light detection and ranging) 193–8, 221–2, 227
lightning strikes 4
limes
  bumblebees 76–7
  climate change 79–80, 87–8, 89–90, 94, 100
  drought response 95
  Georgia 142
  Henry's lime 212
  Kew collection 3, 10, 75–6, 81
  Romania 173, 175
Liquidambar 119
Living Collections Strategy 70
London plane 43, 155
London Urban Forest Partnership 244
London Urban Forest Plan 245
London Urban Resilience Project 97
Loudon, John Claudius 8, 111
'Love Lane' 186

Lucombe oak 56–7
Lucombe, William 56
Luma apiculata 187
Lumberjills 34–5

Macao News 69–70
Magnolia campbellii 11
Magnolia Glade 11
Magnolia x *soulangeana* 90
Mahonia nitens 'Cabaret' 189
maidenhair fern 146
maidenhair tree 4, 145–7, 228–38
Malheur National Forest 102
manna ash 131
maples 10, 119
   Balkan 141, 172
   Cappadocian 130
   field 131–2
   silver 102
Martin, Kevin
   awards 243
   background 73
   Barron's tree transplanter 220
   carbon biomass 223, 226
   development plans 167–8
   joins Kew 73–4
   media interviews 69, 98–9
   microclimate monitoring 59, 63
   research 79–84, 85–9, 91–2, 95–7, 99–101, 114, 175–6, 246–7, 248
   role overview 59–60
   seed collection 119–20, 122, 123, 129, 130, 210
   tree climbing 133
Masson, Francis 7
mast years 172
Mattheck, Claus 108
McCarthy, Dan 152–3
media team 69
Mediterranean cypress 121
Mediterranean Garden 186, 188
Mediterranean medlar 139
medlars 139
Meliosma cuneifolia 4

Merrist Wood College, Guildford 25, 39, 74
Mespilus germanica 139
Metasequoia glyptostroboides 208
Metcalf, Alex 59
Meteorological Office 61
MEWP (mobile elevated work platform) 235–6
microclimates 60–1, 63–4
Millennium Seed Bank (MSB) 123, 125–6, 169
Milne-Redhead, Edgar 166
mistletoe 186
Moat, Justin 193–4, 195, 196–7, 221–2, 223, 226–7
moisture response 59, 60–1, 65, 83, 94–6, 132
monkey puzzles 206
Montezuma's pine 90
moths 44–53
MRT (moving rope technique) 19, 20
MSB (Millennium Seed Bank) 123, 125–6, 169
mulching 149, 151, 152–3, 217
mycorrhizal fungi 153
Myerscough College 245

National Botanical Garden of Georgia (NBGG) 122, 125
National Trust 144, 163
Natural Area 161–3, 165–7, 198, 202, 211
nectar 76–7
needle blights 62, 193
Neill, Aidan 50
Nesfield, William Andrews 9, 56
news reports 69–70
Nicholson, George 110
Nicoll, Alasdair 51–3
'Nifty Lift' 235–6
Nikko firs 113
Niko Ketskhoveli Institute of Botany (IoB), Ilia State University 122–3, 125–7
noble fir 240

noble lime 88
Nordmann fir 122, 126
northern pin oak 57
Nothofagus 10
Notholithocarpus densiflorus 190
nursery 94
Nursery 173–5

oak processionary moth (OPM) 44–53
oaks
  acorns 57, 94, 119, 171
  acute oak decline 64
  biodiversity 53
  Caucasian 142
  chestnut-leaved 54, 55–6, 71–5, 91, 93
  Chinquapin 96
  climate change 89, 90, 92, 93–4, 96–7
  cork 188–9
  cypress oaks 46
  downy 94
  English 53, 63, 64, 79, 89, 90, 92, 96–7, 122, 198–9
  Georgian 121
  holm 90, 91, 194–5
  Hungarian 94, 154
  hybrids 57
  Kew collection 3, 10, 53–8
  largest acorns 57
  largest volume 55–6
  Lucombe 56–7
  microclimate monitoring 63
  northern pin oak 57
  number of species 55
  pest treatments 45, 47–50
  Pontine 124, 142–3, 171, 242
  root systems 79
  sessile 53, 64
  Turkey 156–9, 160, 163
  Turner's 147–8
Old Lions 4, 6, 106, 145–7, 230
Olea europaea 79
olive tree 79, 91, 121
Oliver's lime 76

Oni, Georgia 124
Openshaw, Isabel 193, 195, 196–7, 221–2, 223, 226–7
Ophiostoma novoulmi 62
Orchard Project 244
oriental beech 94, 130, 131, 133–4, 140
oriental hawthorn 125
oriental hornbeam 130, 131, 140, 142, 175
oriental plane 4, 90
Osborn, Arthur 33, 110
Ostrya carpinifolia 90
Oxford, University of, Botanic Garden 23

Pagoda 9
Pagoda Vista 50, 207, 219, 221
Pales processioneae 52
Palm House 9, 160, 186
palms 186–7
paper plant 187
parasitoids 52
Paris Agreement 84
Parrotia persica 75
pathways 13, 14
Paulownia
  P. fargesii 180
  P. kawakamii 11
pea-light tree 156–60
pears 162, 170
perfumery 211
Persian ironwood 75
pests
  biosecurity 60–1, 134
  Canine Assisted Pest Eradication 62
  oak processionary moth (OPM) 44–53
  UK arrivals 61–3
PET (potential evapotranspiration) 83, 85
phloem vessels 59
photosynthesis 58, 94–5, 153
Phytophthora amorum 62
Phytophthora ramorum 241

Picea 141–2, 206–7
  P. abies 'Laxa' 63
  P. koyamae 209
  P. orientalis 122
  P. schrenkiana 180
  P. sitchensis 240
pines 207
  black 28, 193–5, 196–8, 221–3
  Corsican 4
  Montezuma's 90
Pinetum 9, 10, 60, 168, 204–9, 210, 211
pinetums 28
Pinus 207
  P. coulteri 204
  P. monetzumae 90
  P. nigra 28, 193–5, 196–8, 221–3
  P. nigra subsp. *laricio* 4
  P. pinaster 205
  P. ponderosa 205
  P. sylvestris 122
planes 4, 43, 90, 155
plant-identification tests 185–91, 192–3
planting trees 210, 211–12, 213–17
Platanus
  P. x *hispanica* 43
  P. orientalis 4, 90
Plumpton College, Brighton 22
Plymouth pear 162
podocarps 207
Polish larch 210, 211, 213
pollution 207
Polylepis australis 190
Pontine oak 124, 142–3, 171, 242
poplars 164–7
Populus
  P. nigra subsp. *betuliflora* 164–7
  P. tremuloides 81
potato blight 62
potatoes, baking in compost 154
potential evapotranspiration (PET) 83, 85
propagation 137, 210
protective clothing 18, 29, 103
pruning 105, 107–8, 234–8
Prunus 9

P. avium 131
P. cerasifera 131
P. spinosa 125
Pseudotsuga
  P. japonica 209
  P. menziesii 240
Pyrus
  P. communis 170
  P. cordata 162

Quarter Sawn mill, Edale 154
Queen's Cottage Grounds 54, 161–2
Queens Park, London 52
Quercus
  Kew collection 3, 10
  Q. alnifolia 57
  Q. castaneifolia 55–6, 249
  Q. cerris 156–9
  Q. frainetto 154
  Q. x *hispanica* 'Lucombeana 56–7
  Q. ilex 90, 91, 194–5
  Q. insignis 57
  Q. x *kewensis* 57
  Q. macranthera 142, 171
  Q. petraea 53
  Q. petraea subsp. *polycarpa* 121
  Q. pontica 124, 142–3, 171, 242
  Q. prinoides 96
  Q. robur 53, 198–9
  Q. robur 'Fastigiata Koster' 46
  Q. suber 188–9
  Q. x *turneri* 147–8
  Q. urbani 90

Raffill's Walk 157
rainfall 83, 85–6
Raymond Gubbay Limited 156
red-necked longhorn beetle 62
redwoods 4, 90, 207, 208, 239
removing trees 5, 12–13, 14, 15, 16, 177–8, 194–5, 198, 223–6
rescue training 28
research
  climate adaptation 69, 75, 77–8, 79–84, 85–9

INDEX

limes and bees 76–7
  microclimates and disease 60–1
retrenching 231
Reuters 69
Rhododendron caucasicum 141
Richmond Borough 165
risk assessments 199–200
Riverside Walk 155
Robinia pseudoacacia 4
Robshaw, Nellie 33
rock-climbing 21
Romania 93, 173, 175
root systems 79
ropes and rigging 15, 17–19, 72
ropes and rigging for tree removal 112
Rose Garden 11
roses 139
Royal Botanic Garden Edinburgh 24–5, 210, 238–9
Royal Horticultural Society (RHS) 31, 135, 144
Royal Parks 165
Royal Parks Guild Apprenticeship Discovery Day 144–50
Rubus cockburnianus 190
Ruined Arch 190

safety
  climbing techniques 20–1, 23–4, 112
  protective clothing 18, 29, 103
  pruning 235
  risk assessments 199–200
  tree removal 5, 13, 14, 17–18
Salix alba 140
saplings 165, 166, 167, 210, 212
sapphire dragon tree 11
saucer magnolia 90
scanning trees with LiDAR 193–8, 221–2, 227
Sciadopitys 207
Science Strategy 247
Scots pine 122
Second World War 34

seed collection
  cold stratification and dormancy 172–3
  cut test 171–2
  Georgia 119–20, 122–6, 129–34, 138–44, 167–8, 170
  humid, temperate locations 90
  mast years 172
  semi-arid locations 91, 92–3
  sink tests 134, 171
seeds
  orthodox 169–70
  recalcitrant 57, 169–70
Selwyn House 154
Sequoia 207
  S. sempervirens 4, 208
Sequoiadendron giganteum 239
service tree 132
sessile oak 53, 64
Shigo, Alex 107–8
shop products at Kew 154–5
Sikharulidze, Shalva 'Nukri' 122, 123, 124, 127, 143
silver birch 89
silver fir 239
silver lime 76, 88, 95
silver maple 102
Simpson, Jamie 165
sink tests 134, 171
Sitka spruce 240
Sjöman, Henrik 99–100, 120, 122–4, 129–30, 131, 132, 169, 210
Skimmia x *confusa* 'Kew Green' 189
Sky News 69
Slater, Duncan 234
Slessor, Jamie
  Abies research 112–13
  background 14–15
  carbon biomass 223
  deadwooding 199, 200, 203
  Discovery Days 145–50
  pea-light tree 157–8
  pruning 107
  on soil quality 148, 149
  stump removal 103

tree removal 177
small-leaved gum 177
Smeaton, John 81
Smith, John 8, 206
soil aeration 35, 41, 148–9
soil compaction 86–7
soil quality at Kew 148, 149–50
sonic tomography 41–2
Sorbus
  S. aria 162
  S. torminalis 132
southern beech 10
Sparsholt College, Winchester 38, 73
Spatial Analysis and Data Science 193
spindle tree 131
spoon oak 90
spruces 122, 206–7, 209, 240
SRT (stationary rope technique) 19–20
stage beetles 162
stakes 217
Staphylea colchica 170
steppe environments 93, 130, 176
Stevenson, Phil 76–7, 78
stomata 79, 94–5
stone pines 205, 221
Storm Bert 176–7
Storm Darragh 180
Storm Éowyn 238–9, 241–2
stress 94
Stuart, John, 3rd Earl of Bute 6
stump removal 102–4
Styphnolobium japonicum 4, 138, 145
Styrax japonicus 58
subsidence 245
Summers, Alex 69
sustainability 82, 104, 154–5, 168
Sustainability Strategy (2021) 82, 104
Swanley Horticultural College 31
sweet chestnut 24–5, 142, 162, 221, 239
sycamores 119
symbiosis 153
Syon Vista 56, 91

tachinid flies 52
tanbark oak 190

tar on pruning wounds 106, 108
taxonomy 113, 205
Tbilisi, Georgia 123, 127–9, 137
temperature, urban heat island effect 97–9
temperature response 59, 60–1, 63, 83, 85, 97–8
Terravent 148
Thames 9
Thaumetopoea processionea 44–53
Thiselton-Dyer, William 31
Thorn Avenue 186
Thuja 207
  T. plicata 154
Tilia
  bumblebees 76–7
  climate change 79–80, 87–8, 94
  Kew collection 3, 10, 75–6
  T. americana 88
  T. chinensis 88
  T. cordata 79–80
  T. dasystyla 75, 88, 142, 245
  T. x europaea 89–90
  T. henryana 212
  T. kiusiana 88
  T. nobilis 88
  T. oliveri 76, 88
  T. platyphyllos 88
  T. tomentosa 76, 95, 173, 175, 245
timber products 154–5, 164
Toomer, Simon 69, 245
Torreya 207
Trachycarpus fortunei 186–7
traits and climate change 78–9, 80, 91–2, 95–6, 100
transpiration 64–5, 83, 85, 95
transplanting 217–21
tree assessments 37, 39–42, 229, 231–4
Tree Council 144, 145, 146
Tree Gang *see also* Church, Rich; Demain, Sal; Fry, Tom; Gregg, Arthur; Harding, Will; Martin, Kevin; Slessor, Jamie; Withall, Cecily
  deadwooding 199–203

INDEX

planning work 35–7
pruning 235–8
role overview 11–12
Royal Botanic Garden Edinburgh 239–42
Stable Yard workshop 150–1
stump removal 102–4
tasks overview 35
tree planting 210, 211–12, 213–17
tree removal 13, 14, 15, 16–17, 177–9, 198, 223–6
tree height measurement 43
Tree Listening Project 59
Tree Register of the British Isles 55
tree relocation 56–7
tree removal *see* removing trees
Tree Risk Assessment Qualification 39
Tree Smart software 36–7, 39, 49, 231, 232
tree transplanter 217–21
TreeGoer 83
trees
 Champions 55
 genetic diversity 57–8
 largest volume 55–6
 most endangered 113
 rarest native 164
 tallest 4, 208
Trees for Cities 244
trembling aspen 81
trichomes 79
Tsuga 206
turgor loss point 80, 95–6, 132
Turkey oak 156–9, 160, 163
Turner, Ian 145, 147, 149–50
Turner's oak 147–8

UK National Tree Seed Project 165
umbrella pines 207
understorey 58, 169
United Nations, Paris Agreement 84
University Centre Myerscough 74
University of Central Lancashire 74
University of Exeter 61

University of Oxford, Botanic Garden 23
University Parks 23
urban heat island effect 97–9
urban landscaping 75, 97, 99–101, 132, 244–5
Urban Tree Strategy for Greater London 244
utilities, power lines and trees 38

Vaccinium arctostaphylos 141
vapour pressure deficit 65, 95
Vapour Pressure Osmometers 96
veteranization 163
Victoria 161, 219
Visitor Operations 13
von Meyer, Carl Anton 55, 71

Wakehurst 165
Wallin, Emil 120, 129
walnuts 3
Walpole, Horace 6
Wardian cases 9
water distribution 94–5
water distribution in trees 59, 64–5, 80
 see also drought
'water engine' 81
water fir 208
water run off 86
water supply
 irrigation 81–2
 rainfall 83, 85–6
Waterlily House 11
Watson, William 29, 30, 33
weather station 61, 85–6, 98
weevils 134
western red cedar 154
Weston Global Tree Seed Bank: Unlocked 125–6
Westonbirt Arboretum 23, 28
white willows 140
whitebeam 162
Whitton 6
whortleberry 141
wild garlic 162

wild service tree 132
willows 140
Wilson, Ernest 210
Wilson, Peter 239
winches 199–201, 203
Winter Garden 189
wintersweet 188
Withall, Cecily
  awards 25
  background 24–5, 239–40
  carbon biomass 223, 226
  deadwooding 199, 200–1, 203
  Serbia 210
  tree removal 177, 224–5
Wollemi pine 89, 204, 208–9
women 25–6, 29–35
Women in Arboriculture group 25–6, 35
Women's Forestry Service (WFS) 34
Women's Timber Corps 34
wood chippers 16, 104–5, 177, 222
wood density 80
Woodland Trust 61, 244
work platforms 235
World Heritage Site Management Plan 2020–2025 70–1
World Wide Opportunities on Organic Farms (WWOOF) 24
worms 150
wound healing 108, 232

xylem 59, 80, 95

yellow buckeye 238
yew 206
yews 207, 219

Zelkova carpinifolia 75, 138–9, 142, 143

Acknowledgements

The authors would like to thank the following for their help in the research and writing of this book:

Kew's Tree Gang: Kevin Martin, Tom Fry, Rich Church, Will Harding, Jamie Slessor, Cecily Withall, Arthur Gregg and Sal Demain.

Ruth Brookes, Jake Davies-Robertson and Dan McCarthy in the Kew Arboretum team.

Justin Moat and Isabel Openshaw in the Kew Spatial Analysis and Data Science team.

Kiri Ross-Jones, Isabel Lauterjung and Alice Nelson in the Kew Archives team.

Ben Jones and the team at the University of Oxford Botanic Garden & Harcourt Arboretum.

Dan Luscombe and Dylan Laidler at Bedgebury Pinetum.

Dean Jones, Aidan Neill and Tom Adamson from Bartlett Tree Experts.

Dr Henrik Sjöman and Emil Wallin at the Gothenburg Botanical Garden.

Professor Shalva Sikharulidze and David Kikodze of the Niko Ketskhoveli Institute of Botany, Ilia State University, Tbilisi, Georgia.

Ian Turner of The Tree Council.

Simon Kallow and Lee Oliver at Kew's Millennium Seed Bank.

Professor Mark Nesbitt, Dr Caroline Cornish, Professor Phil Stevenson and Dr China Williams from Kew Science.

Professor Felix Driver, Royal Holloway, University of London.

And for their expert help in the design and production of this book, we are very grateful to:

Jessica Minocha and the editorial team at Octopus Publishing.

Lydia White and the team at Kew Publishing.

Jeff Eden and Ines Stuart-Davidson from Kew's Creative Studio.

About Kew Gardens

The Royal Botanic Gardens, Kew is a world-famous scientific and horticultural institution and conservation charity, whose mission is to understand and protect plants and fungi for the well-being of people and the future of all life on Earth. It is internationally respected for its outstanding collections, horticultural and scientific expertise in plant and fungal diversity, conservation and sustainable development in the UK and around the globe.

Kew Gardens, with its 130 hectares (320 acres) of historic, landscaped gardens, is a major attraction for visitors from around the world. Dating back to 1759, the site has a rich history and was made a UNESCO World Heritage Site in July 2003. Combined visitor numbers with Wakehurst, Kew's wild botanic garden in Sussex, total over 2.5 million per year. Wakehurst is home to the Millennium Seed Bank, the largest wild plant seed bank in the world and a safeguard against the worst effects of climate change and biodiversity loss.

Kew receives approximately one-third of its funding from the UK Government through the Department for the Environment, Food and Rural Affairs (Defra) and research councils, with the remaining two-thirds coming from supporters, sponsors, memberships and commercial activity, including ticket sales. This enables Kew to carry out its vital scientific and educational work. Visit the official Kew website http://www.kew.org for more information about Kew's work and how to visit Kew Gardens and Wakehurst.

Picture Credits

1a, 1b, 3a, 5b, 7a, 9b, 16a Jeff Eden © RBG Kew; 2a, 2b, 5a, 9c, 15a © RBG Kew; 3b, 4a, 10a, 10b, 10c, 13d Carolyn Fry; 4b, 8b, 9a Christina Harrison; 6a, 6b, 7b, 8a, 13a, 13b, 13c, 14a, 14b, 15b, 16b Ines Stuart-Davidson © RBG Kew; 11a, 11b, 12a, 12b Tom Fry.